First Lady of Tennis
HAZEL HOTCHKISS WIGHTMAN

First Lady of Tennis
Hazel Hotchkiss Wightman

by
Tom Carter

CREATIVE ARTS BOOK COMPANY
Berkeley • California

Copyright © 1997 by James M. Hotchkiss, Jr.
Copyright © 2001 by James M. Hotchkiss, Jr.

No part of this book may be reproduced in any manner without written permission from the publisher, except in brief quotations used in articles or reviews.

First Lady of Tennis: Hazel Hotchkiss Wightman
is published by Donald S. Ellis
and distributed by Creative Arts Book Company

For information contact:
Creative Arts Book Company
833 Bancroft Way
Berkeley, California 94710
1-800-848-7789

ISBN 0-88739-334-9
Library of Congress Catalog Number 99-06985

Printed in the United States of America

TABLE OF CONTENTS

Preface vii

Introduction ix

Chapter 1
Family, Childhood 1

Chapter 2
Tennis Beginnings 6

Chapter 3
May Sutton and Tennis Triumphs 11

Chapter 4
Marriage, Talent Scouting and Helen Wills 33

Chapter 5
The Wightman Cup 42

Chapter 6
Life with George, the 1924 Olympics 48

Photo Section 57

Chapter 7
Sarah Palfrey 101

Chapter 8
Lady Houseguests, West Visits East 106

Chapter 9
    Hazel's Garage 114

Chapter 10
    Teaching the English, the Evolving Wightman Cup . . 121

Chapter 11
    Modern Players, Modern Costumes 128

Chapter 12
    Hazel's Descendants 137

Chapter 13
    Honors 145

Appendix A.
    Wightman Cup Players 151

Appendix B.
    Major Titles Won by Hazel 157

Appendix C.
    Sources 159

Appendix D.
    Museums and Exhibitions 161

    Better Tennis -*Hazel Hotchkiss Wightman* 163

PREFACE

To me she was always "Aunt Hazel", my father's sister. Even though we lived three thousand miles apart, I got to know her during her regular summer long visits with my grandfather and grandmother. It was a well traveled path. My parents took me to Boston in 1935 and again in 1940. Hazel continued to come west on an irregular basis after her parents died. I knew her as a child knows an adult until 1948. In that year I came to Boston at the age of twenty-one with my beautiful new bride. "I want you to meet my famous Aunt Hazel," I told Isabel.

That was when I was introduced to something special. I did not know that my visit was coincidental with the national doubles championship. Isabel and I had to stay at a hotel while Aunt Hazel's house was occupied by a horde of young lady tennis players. Of course, we were permitted to watch the tennis matches, hear Hazel give a speech, and visit after the tennis in Hazel's house. Several things really impressed me about my aunt. She ran the house like a little general. Laundry and meals were very carefully scheduled. Of course, there was always time to serve freshly baked brownies. Incredibly, she saved personal time for Isabel and me. We got to know her well right in the midst of what rightfully should have been chaos.

What impressed me more than anything else was the reverence shown toward my aunt by the many tennis players, senior and junior. They were all fond of her and very respectful. I discovered that she was a superstar on and off the court. I saw Hazel many times thereafter and had the pleasure of bringing my children to Boston. They were treated to a tennis lesson in the garage, like thousands before them.

There have been several biographical articles written about my aunt, but there has never been a whole book. Also, it has been over two decades since she died. A new generation has come along that never met her, and they should be given the opportunity to know her. Hazel's daughter, Dorothy (Cousin Dotty to me) and I saw an opportunity when we got to know Tom Carter, who knew the world of tennis and had a real feeling for Hazel and her importance to the game. Dotty and I persuaded Tom to write the biography, and we are pleased that he was able to capture Hazel's spirit so well.

It was my idea to combine the new biography in one volume with Better Tennis, the book that Hazel wrote in 1933. Readers who know tennis will notice that some of Hazel's teachings have been superceded by more modern thoughts. How to hold the racket and serving (They changed the serving rules!) are examples. However, the instructions on how to cooperate with your partner are timeless.

Aunt Hazel played hard, but she played by the rules. Whenever she stepped on the court, she gave her maximum effort. Afterwards she was gracious whether she won or lost. That attitude permeates Better Tennis. I think it is a pretty good attitude for anybody to have sixty-seven years later.

Jim Hotchkiss

INTRODUCTION

Lawn tennis, invented by the British a scant twenty-seven years before the turn of the twentieth century, was not yet crawling out of its cozy American bassinet in 1900.

As in England, the sport in America was a cosset of the rich. Besides being played on private estates, it was found behind the imposing gates of country clubs and at towering resort hotels with their gingerbread architecture. These bastions of privilege were the summertime settings of mannered, pitty-pat recreations and also of brisk regional and national tennis tournaments. Such locales did little to accelerate the acceptance of lawn tennis as a bona fide sport. Access to lawn tennis was beyond the means of middle-class America in most sections of the country.

To be sure, the game by then was deeply loved if very much turned inward. If the players wanted more people to know what a terrific sport tennis was, they didn't promote it very ardently; they were just learning how to dote on it themselves. Teaching the basics, or stroke fundamentals, just wasn't anything anyone did. People worked their tennis shots out on their own. Serious teaching would have involved an odor of professionalism, not admired by the upper classes. Passing along a few pointers among friends was okay, though, because it was all for the love of the game, the amateur game.

In the main, the world of sports was nobly, if not gloriously, amateur in thought and deed. Respect for the unwritten rules of manners and tradition, was as important as respect for the written rules. There was a lot of talk about the spirit of sport itself, its purity, and how it brought people together and promoted goodwill. The reborn Olympics were endeavoring to prove that sports were, or could be, the zenith of it all.

A sense of nationalism was budding. Davis Cup competition, which embodied an international dream, began as a small affair in 1900 at the Longwood Cricket Club in Boston. It was a showdown with only two teams, the British challenging the Americans, who were the originators and donors of the cup. The Americans won.

Most tennis was played on grass. The official game, after all, dated back to the liberating Major Wingfield of England, who had brought indoor, wall-bounded court tennis out onto a plain open lawn for guests at a pheasant shoot at Nantclwyd Hall in 1873. He called the game "Sphairistike." The arbitrary boundary lines he drew for a court were in the shape of an hourglass. Across the narrow middle of the court the major stretched a net that stood four feet eight inches high. Players used hollow rubber balls and larger, thicker rackets than badminton frames, and they played inside a larger court area. Under a patent obtained in February 1874, Major Wingfield packaged and sold complete tennis kits. The activity was touted by one magazine for the landed gentry as an ideal "out-of-door amusement at country houses." It was also considered suitable to be played on ice, until practical experience proved otherwise. Women were thought a bit too delicate for the game.

Ironically, a woman, Mary Outerbridge of Staten Island, often gets credit for bringing tennis to America. Vacationing in Bermuda in 1874, she saw some English officers playing it and brought one of the kits to America. By the late 1870s courts had been set up at clubs in Brookline, Massachusetts, Newport, Rhode Island, and Philadelphia.

Tennis reached California in 1879 according to newspaper accounts. The William Allen family, part of an English contingent settling in the Pasadena area, was spending the hot summer months at the seashore. They had brought along one of those unique "portable court" tennis kits. William met Canadian-born and Oxford-educated William Young, who had recently settled in Santa Monica after winning a tournament in the south of France. The two men set up a crude net on an unpaved Santa Monica street. "And in the dust was played, as far as is known," says a 1948 *Christian Science Monitor* story, "the first game in Southern California."

Outing magazine quoted a different origination time in Northern California. In its July 1890 issue, it reported that "Lawn tennis came to

California in October 1880, when some English businessmen began a club at San Rafael near San Francisco and put in turf courts." Possibly, play on another surface existed elsewhere in the Bay Area before 1880. It is known that before the turn of the century Indians in Marin County sold crushed seashells by the basketful to independent court makers who were devising a form of dirt court.

The United States National Lawn Tennis Association (USNLTA) grew out of a need, among others, to standardize courts and equipment. The move to create the USNLTA, now known simply as the USTA, was spearheaded by James Dwight of Boston, often called the father of American tennis. Dwight, a Harvard-educated doctor, was a short man of about five feet six inches but a good athlete. As a graduate student, he had brought a tennis kit to America from Europe about the same time Mary Outerbridge brought hers. Dwight played avidly in the earliest tournaments but boycotted the singles of one event on Staten Island because the balls were lighter, smaller, and softer than the ones called for under the regulations he played by. The net might be six inches higher in one city than in another, too, for rules varied all over the place.

Dwight was one of three people who called for an organizational meeting in May 1881 to standardize such things. The other two men were Emelius Outerbridge of Staten Island (Mary's youngest brother) and Clarence M. Clark of Philadelphia. The resulting convention on May 21, 1881, attracted representatives from nineteen clubs, and fifteen others were represented by proxies. None were west of Pittsburgh, Pennsylvania. Dwight and Outerbridge ran the meeting, and the United States National Lawn Tennis Association was created. In 1882, borrowing a bit from the British standards, the USNLTA adopted court and ball specifications that stand today. Dwight eventually went on to hold every office in the association.

Compared to the East and its shower-laced summers, California was a terrible place to try to grow turf for tennis. California didn't have the seasonal rainfall or the proper soil. Regardless, the rate at which Californians took up "lawn" tennis may have excelled the eastern surge. That's because Californians could play year-round. *Outing* magazine estimated that fifty vigorous clubs up and down the California coast had sprouted by 1890. By then, both Northern and Southern California were on their way to becoming the forerunners of practical, low-maintenance hard courts made of asphalt and cement.

California's municipal park and recreation departments were also taking a hard look at tennis. John McClaren, who did the major planning for Golden Gate Park, thought it was a perfect game for families, and so one of the nation's first great public tennis facilities was begun there in 1894 with two dirt courts and a wood clubhouse.

Already, though, tennis was shaded by a derogatory public reputation, especially in the East. That tennis should be ridiculed as a bauble of the rich was understandable. But it suffered because it had somehow become known as "a woman's game." The early British view that women were too delicate for tennis had been superseded by the suspicion that tennis might be too delicate for men. It was true that it was a wonderfully athletic game that women could play. But that shouldn't have implied it was therefore a less demanding game for men. Away from the courts, tennis simply was not very well understood. It took an image-beating that lasted for decades.

Women were more constrained in the sport than men, both physically because of the kinds of clothing they wore and socially because of custom. Women were supposed to adhere to a concept of femininity that held them poised and reserved in their pursuits, never too aggressive, never rumpled or unsightly in public. Moreover, in a male-dominated society, women didn't have equal opportunities to develop their skills in tennis. No one stepped forward to help them along, either.

Marion Jones outlined the women's problems in a 1900 interview in London with *Lawn Tennis and Badminton* magazine. Jones was twenty at the time. Her father had struck it rich in silver in Nevada's Comstock Lode in 1879. He bought a large land parcel in the Santa Monica area and built a mansion there. He founded the city, in fact. Because of ill health, Marion was brought as a child to their new home on a stretcher. She regained her strength through tennis, which she played on the Santa Monica Casino courts.

Miss Jones went on to win the 1899 U.S. women's singles held at the Philadelphia Cricket Club. (The men played at the Newport Casino in Rhode Island.) Actually, Miss Jones won the final by default, becoming the only one in history to do so. In 1890, she was reportedly the first American woman to play Wimbledon, losing in the quarterfinals. Then she was on her way to Paris to study music. (No one would have made the long sea voyage to Europe and back just to play in the All-England Championships at Wimbledon.) In Paris, she became the first American to enter the Olympic tennis competition, and she earned a bronze medal in women's singles.

Miss Jones told her British interviewer that American women would have little chance in a showdown against the more skillful and experienced English ladies. The chief reason the American ladies were handicapped, she said, was because the major men's and women's tournaments were played apart from each other. "I think that tennis in America would be greatly improved if the principal tournaments for men and women were not separated," she said. "It would make all the difference in the world to the girls who would [then] have the opportunity of studying the play of the men."

Another thing holding women back, she said, was travel time and the expense involved in playing major tournaments. The American Nationals were played on the East's grass courts. Traveling from California to New York took four and a half days by train. It was thirty hours from New York to Chicago. "Indeed," she said, "I have often wondered at the enthusiasm which has prompted so many girls to go such vast distances simply to get a chance of learning, partly by meeting girls who have had better opportunities, and partly by watching the men." Miss Jones said she thought girls from such big cities as Chicago and Philadelphia had the best chance of improving. They had country clubs where tournaments were held and where good practice could be lined up. "But they [the clubs] are all too expensive for most girls," she said. "The girl who is not so favorably situated spends all her allowance on writing letters and traveling expenses in getting a few games with a few good players. Almost the only place that I know of where a girl can have a professional to teach her is at Kenwood near Chicago, where the courts are excellent."

Another obstacle was that American men, as mannerly as they were, were not anxious to share a court with women, even in the cause of mixed doubles. In an 1893 edition of a book he wrote on tennis, James Dwight had said: "It may be taken for granted that the lady is not as strong a player as her partner, and the game therefore consists in protecting your own partner and attacking your adversary's." To that he added glumly, "Ladies' and gentlemen's doubles is not a game that I can speak of with much respect."

Miss Jones pointed out to her interviewer that mixed doubles weren't so popular in America as they were in England. "It is probably because the men don't care to play with inferior partners," Miss Jones said, "and this, of course, tends to keep girls down as much as anything.

"Tennis is very largely kept up by men's universities, but the courts are not open to women. The fact is, that if a girl who wishes to improve does not know another girl of about her equal in skill living somewhere near her, she has next to no chance of getting any better. So, many girls who would play well if they had the chance are obliged to content themselves with playing others whom they can beat so easily that it is no practice for them."

Girls' schools and colleges weren't much help. "I am sorry to say that in most of them only basketball is played at present, although a very few encourage lawn tennis in the spring and fall," Miss Jones explained. "But for three months during the summer when the lawn tennis season is at its height, the colleges are closed and the girls go always to the seaside with their families."

In the West, though, things were about to change. A dominant women's champion, May Sutton, would emerge from Southern California to become the best in the world. The intensity of women's play was destined to heat up very soon when she was challenged in the sport's first classic women's rivalry. The diminutive antagonist was Hazel Hotchkiss from the North. Their tight-lipped tussling involved a new contrast of distinct styles, the forerunners of styles that are in evidence even now in women's tennis at the highest professional level: the blistering ground game versus the aggressive net game.

Hazel Hotchkiss can be said to have actually invented an entirely new style of play for women. She dared to play like a man. She went on to become the Queen Mother of women's tennis of the twentieth century as Hazel Hotchkiss Wightman, founder of the Wightman Cup.

Committed completely to the game for her lifetime as a player, volunteer teacher, and diplomat, she was like an Eleanor Roosevelt of tennis. For over half a century, she profoundly influenced leading players from one coast to the other, guiding them, teaching them, even housing and feeding them. And it was not just to the proficient, elite players that she gave herself. She went into the schools and universities and parks to sow the seed of tennis among thousands. Her mission lasted until her death at age eighty-seven in 1974. Her contribution will never be matched.

First Lady of Tennis
HAZEL HOTCHKISS WIGHTMAN

Chapter 1

FAMILY, CHILDHOOD

When Hazel Hotchkiss was born on December 20, 1886, there was absolutely no reason to predict that she would become a historic figure in the world's first great rivalry among women tennis players, that she would marry into a prominent Boston family, or that she would spend her life advancing the cause of women in tennis.

Her childhood was rural, spent in an idyllic environment on the family farm, 375 acres near Healdsburg, California, where she was surrounded by her parents and four brothers. In this pastoral setting, the family nonetheless managed to provide an atmosphere of competitiveness and high-hearted risk-taking that must have been a major factor in her later confidence as a tennis innovator.

The Hotchkiss family tree, with its roots planted firmly in England, has been for several years the engrossing hobby of Jim Hotchkiss, the son of Hazel Hotchkiss's brother, James Miller Hotchkiss.

Jim Hotchkiss is a certified public accountant and financial planner with his own practice in Orinda, a small East Bay commuter community dotted with Spanish architecture. He has come to love the odd behaviors and historical anecdotes of courage and business acumen he has discovered in his predecessors. Telling a favorite story, he'll sit back, fold his hands primly on his ample stomach, and spin out a yarn in a slow cadence, savoring the telling like hard candy. If he scores at the end with a droll punch line his face squeezes into a closed-mouth grin so broad and tight his eyes disappear.

"You think of pedigrees and strong lineage that you associate with certain names in the East," he says. "The Wightmans go back to an ancestor I call Edward the Burned. He was the last martyr to be burned at the stake in England. But I always thought it was rather interesting that George Wightman, with his fancy Wightman pedigree, met a girl from the Wild West where the Indians live, and her pedigree was as long as his, although I don't think any of them knew it at the time. I didn't discover it until thirty years ago."

Through the Hotchkiss Family Association, Jim was delighted to trace the family roots back to England, several generations preceding Benoni Hotchkiss, Hazel's pioneer grandfather, who crossed the plains by covered wagon in 1860.

The beginning of the American line was Samuel Hotchkiss, who arrived in the New Haven colony at age fifteen in 1638 and got his share of the new lands that were opening up. Samuel courted Elizabeth Cleverly, origin unknown. "But they were people just like everybody else," Jim Hotchkiss says, adding that they were subject to the colony's many petty fines and punishments for such minor infractions as owning a rusty gun or having a dirty chimney (a fire hazard). From a colony report Hotchkiss knows the two youngsters were accused of a "filthy dalliance" and were "severely whipped" by the authorities. "The next day they asked for permission to be married," Jim says, "even though they were underage."

Six generations later, Benoni Hotchkiss and his family left Campbellsville, Kentucky, to catch a wagon train in Missouri bound for the West. They were part of the migration era, when more than three hundred thousand crossed the plains following the Oregon Trail. Traveling two thousand miles, they settled in Healdsburg, California, to begin farming. Their son, W. J. (initials were a popular style then), was two years old. He eventually courted a neighbor's daughter, Emma Grove, whose family had migrated from Virginia by train, and married her. "It's a long way to get across the other guy's property when you just have a horse and buggy," Jim Hotchkiss points out. "And you took what you got."

W. J. and Emma, nicknamed Gaga, had five children: Miller (Jim's father), Homer, Marius, Linville, and Hazel. To Jim Hotchkiss, although he thought the world of his Aunt Hazel, W. J. was the shining light in this chain. "He never got the publicity he deserved," Jim says.

W. J. was a promoter-developer, a wheeler-dealer bent on exciting the men who played money games, a turn-of-the-century venture capitalist who made a million dollars—and lost it. Funny and witty, he gathered ideas, selected the best, went out and borrowed money, started things, and then was on to other projects.

He was a Healdsburg high school graduate who took some business courses and then taught school but didn't care for it. There was money in farming, and the family did have 375 acres, so W. J. went into the prune-drying business in the 1880s with a neighbor. The venture went bust and the neighbor moved to Washington. The undismayed W. J. kept on with his bright ideas and settled on canning. This worked better. In time, W. J. created the largest canning company in California, Central California Canneries, which operated sixteen canning plants throughout Northern California. When another group was struggling to merge as Cal Pak, W. J. threw his lot in behind it in 1916 and made it a success. They called this vast amalgamation Del Monte Corporation and made W. J. president.

"He was always flitting from place to place checking on business interests," Jim Hotchkiss says. "He never drove. He was driven, first by buggy, then by car. Once he was going through a little town and abruptly told the driver to stop. He disappeared inside a bank and came out smiling. He said, 'Only bank I've seen where I haven't borrowed money.' The driver asked if he had gotten some; W. J. nodded yes and they drove on." Hotchkiss smiles. "People revered W. J. Even when he borrowed money from them and couldn't pay it back, they still liked him."

W. J. didn't stay Del Monte's president long. He went on to other ventures, such as Hotchkiss Redwood Co. and the Hobbs-Wall Lumber Co. way up in Del Norte County. This was about the time the Golden Gate Bridge District was formed. A major advocate of building the span, W. J. became a powerful member of the spearheading Bridging The Golden Gate Association. He was elected chairman of its executive committee, which chose the architect, Joseph Strauss, and he was responsible for bringing in a key Del Norte County vote to approve the bridge. "It's quite possible that there never would have been a Golden Gate Bridge, or that its construction might have been delayed for decades but for the efforts of my grandfather," Hotchkiss says.

W. J. and Gaga set a high standard of excellence and expected their children to attain it. "They wanted their children to be successful, and as a result the children were intensely competitive with one another," Hotchkiss says. "It showed up in little things and it showed up in the tennis. Hazel was fiercely competitive but had all the integrity that any person of integrity can have. She wouldn't lie, cheat, or steal. But she sure as hell would lob into the sun."

As a young child, she had been prone to headaches, but it was found that if she got outside and was physically active in the fresh air, her health was excellent. In fact, it was there among her brothers and youngsters from adjacent ranches that she developed into a good athlete and a popular one. She was always one of the first chosen in scrub baseball. And when her brothers wanted to shag flies, they asked her to bat. She could toss the ball up and knock it solidly into the outfield like no other girl they had seen. She was adept at pole-vaulting over barbed wire fences, too. But it was any kind of ball game that she felt comfortable with, and she was very keen to compete. Her sickliness all but disappeared.

No doubt she got her calculating, risk-taking proclivities from her father, and possibly her stamina from her mother. The four brothers had more of W. J.'s sense of humor than Hazel had. But she had her father's shrewdness, along with a dogged stamina from her mother, a demanding woman who people thought was practically humorless. It's a family story that when Gaga, a Christian Scientist, once broke her leg she sequestered herself in her room and didn't come out until the leg had healed enough to walk on. Time lapsed: two days.

Hazel's mother also threw herself entirely into projects and expected a rewarding return. She was such a strong Democrat it was rumored she had given all her inheritance money to the party during the Woodrow Wilson administration. She was a delegate to the 1924 Democratic convention. It was further rumored that she was a candidate for Postmaster General when Franklin Delano Roosevelt was first elected in 1933.

Likely, Hazel was adept in getting along in a man's world not just because she had four brothers but because of W. J.'s example. It was probable, too, that W. J. looked forward to escorting his only daughter east for her tournament triumphs, because his relationship with his wife was somewhat strained.

Getting away from home was as much respite as adventure. Jim Hotchkiss says one family anecdote has W. J. delivering this one-liner to his wife: "I'll do whatever you want if you will just continue to stay in your half of the house."

The Great Depression wrecked W. J.'s creative financial web. "He had done it all on borrowed money, all his life," Hotchkiss reveals. "There was a time when he wrote out a stack of deeds to the Bank of America. He just went through signing them all and a bank representative took them away. He was completely wiped out in 1931. Apartment buildings, all of it.

"He wanted to build these pyramids—his world—and he found he could do it better with a lot of borrowed money than if he did it smaller. It was his way of having fun. If he had been more cautious, it would've been a different story."

W. J. died in 1936 just before the Golden Gate Bridge was completed but well after his daughter had gained another new and different round of international recognition and esteem in the tennis world. Eventually, she ended up building an uncommonly wide base of beginners at tennis' grass roots level while also influencing the world's best players. That was her pyramid.

Chapter 2

TENNIS BEGINNINGS

IN 1900 THE HOTCHKISSES MOVED FROM THEIR 375-ACRE HEALDSBURG FARM TO Berkeley, 75 miles southeast. This was so W. J. could be closer to his San Francisco office and so the four boys—Miller (six years older than Hazel), Homer (four older), Marius (two older), and Linville (two younger)—and Hazel, who was in high school, could go to the University of California, Berkeley.

Hazel was forbidden to play outside their new home on the pavements with her competitive brothers for fear the petite young girl would get hurt. They all played rough. But staying inside wasn't any good for her, either. Her headaches returned. Soon she was pulled out of school because of them. The family doctor prescribed lots of fresh air, exactly what had cured the malady in Healdsburg.

"Then it happened that my brothers, who had played a little tennis, and had taken to it enthusiastically, took me to San Rafael to see a match between the famous Sutton sisters, May and Florence, and we all decided then and there that this would be an excellent game for me," Hazel wrote in her 1933 book *Better Tennis* (which is dedicated to "the young tennis players of California and Massachusetts").

Hazel set aside any qualms she might have had about interminable rallies to win points from the backcourt and commenced practicing on the gravel in her backyard. The uneven bounces were awful. She told her brother Homer that the game would be more interesting if occasionally the ball was hit before it bounced. Homer pointed out that sure, that was a more varied and fast-paced style, but it was aggressive and really a man's way of playing. Nevertheless, sensing her natural desire for this riskier approach, Homer took her then to a men's doubles match that featured Northern California's famous Hardy brothers, Sam and Sumner, the reigning Pacific Coast doubles champions. And to her, these boys were nothing less than the bee's knees.

"The men were very attractive and they looked good moving quickly and smoothly to the net and volleying," she recalled to *American Heritage* magazine in an interview four months before she died. "I loved it! So I said, why not volley the ball, see? And that means you get it back into play quicker. But nobody happened to tell me that. I learned by hitting the ball and having fun. I wasn't contaminated by some teacher telling me just how to do it—hitting the ball this way, or making my racket head come down this way or that way. I didn't think about those things. I just learned to do what I needed to do to make it successful, to make the ball go where I wanted it to go."

She attacked practice with a newfound enthusiasm, focusing first and foremost now on the volley. Her experience might even be a lesson for contemporary youngsters who would be considered late starters at age fifteen or sixteen. Learning to volley first might be best.

"I immediately tried to play the same way [as the men] on our makeshift court in the backyard with a board for a net," she wrote in her book. "In fact, because the gravel surface made the bounce of the ball uncertain, I tried only to volley to keep the ball in play, which was more fun than having to hunt for it continually among the roses and berry bushes. We used to try to keep the ball going up to forty, fifty, or a hundred times before missing, and I had to develop alertness and balance in order not to miss."

In her newfound love, Hazel enjoyed a favored status as the girl of the family, even from her mother Emma. Hazel and the boys were even allowed to bring their compulsive volleying practice indoors, "where, with the danger of a broken vase or lamp, there was even more crucial need of skill and accuracy," Hazel wrote. When the boys broke something with a tennis ball they were forbidden to bring a racket inside. Hazel, however, got second and third chances.

A favorite practicing place outdoors was against the house between two lovely bay windows. Hazel said that "when one of the boys broke a window, I feared my practicing was over, but an exception was made for me from the general ban, and I was permitted to keep on banging against the house. I worked hard."

Hazel learned to volley well, but she also brought all of her previous ball sense to unusual heights in this sport where a girl barely five feet tall could even compete with grown men if she chose. Hazel had wonderful instincts for the game and loved to try them out. In later years, several of her world-class partners, impressed with her uncanny anticipation, said they thought she could predict precisely where a ball was going just by hearing the pinging sound it made coming off opponents' strings.

Yet to learn the sport properly, access to a court was necessary. One did exist in Berkeley in 1902. It was the property of the University of California, the beacon of higher learning all the Hotchkiss siblings, if they weren't already attending, aspired to. It was an asphalt court open to the public. Except that girls weren't allowed on it after 8 A.M.

To bypass the restriction and get to a typical 6 A.M. session there, a friend of Homer's who made the fourth for doubles would come by and awaken him at five o'clock by jerking a string that hung from the side of the Hotchkiss house. It ran up the side and through a bedroom window to the bed, where it was tied around Homer's big toe. That done, Homer would rouse Marius and Hazel. In *The New Yorker* in 1952, Herbert Warren Wind wrote, "The Hotchkisses would grab apples from the kitchen for breakfast and eat them as they trotted the mile to the court in the ocher light of dawn. These matutinal workouts came to an end at 6:30 when Hazel returned home to practice the piano for an hour before heading for classes at Berkeley High School."

Six months after she took up tennis, Homer and Marius, who along with Miller steadfastly encouraged Hazel, told "Sis" they had entered her in her first tournament, the Bay County Women's Singles and Doubles Championships. The December 1902 event was in San Francisco and sponsored by the Park Commission.

On the ferry ride across San Francisco Bay, Hazel by chance met Mary Ratcliffe, a UC student also bound for the tournament. Both had figured the tournament would assign them a partner, but after talking together they decided they'd just become a team.

They won the tournament without the loss of a set. When Mary served, Hazel, just like a Hardy brother, stood five feet from the net and picked off with a winning volley or leaping smash every ball she could reach. All the teams they played were intimidated by such aggression. After her good serves, and even during rallies, she charged the net at every opportunity. It was startling to see, a spectacle really. And people began to talk. Hazel Hotchkiss was writing the first chapter of the revolution that established men's tactics in the women's game, thus cutting the apron strings that had held women to the baseline for twenty-five years.

They upset the favored defending champions, Eva and Maud Varney, in the final in what the *San Francisco Chronicle* called "the most interesting and scientific women's doubles match yet witnessed on the park courts." Hazel and Mary each won a beautiful cut glass and silver cologne bottle.

The next day, in the singles championship, they both lost in the first round. Hazel went out in straight sets to Eva Varney, who then lost to her sister in the semis. "But what a lot I had learned in those two days!" Hazel exclaimed. And three months later in a rematch, she beat her conqueror handily.

The next year, a friend of her father's built a cement court on the Hotchkiss homestead on Claremont Avenue. The court was very close to where the property ran through to Domingo Avenue, where W. J. eventually gave his three older sons lots to build on. (Much later the road to Domingo became Hazel Road, which survives today.)

Naturally, Hazel and her brothers had unlimited use of the court and she continued to improve and to expand her orbit of tournaments. Seven or eight were an average seasonal load for a serious player. Seldom did Hazel lose in doubles or mixed doubles, and she always attracted attention. She was quite a study, a bright tactician, stoic and all business, a little general. The steely gaze of her blue-gray eyes was implacable, but simultaneously she was bubbling inside with the excitement of every challenging point and its fascinating patterns, then bursting forth with the winning shot. Never, though, was she too self-absorbed to encourage her partner.

Women learned things just by watching Hazel. Men were delighted to share a court with her. She could volley alongside the best of them. Imagine, here was a girl who could not only handle her share of overheads but do so impressively. She became a very popular partner.

Equally capable in singles, in 1904 Hazel won the women's California State singles title. The tournament was held in the North and did not attract many southerners. Travel expenses often hindered draws: unless local families were willing to house players and the tournaments or fledgling associations sponsoring the players could spring for train fares, quality players of modest means chose distant destinations sparingly. But Hazel's finances weren't as dear.

The state title qualified Hazel to be invited to play in tournaments in Portland, Tacoma, Seattle, and Canada, "the northern trip," she called it. She played in seven tournaments that year and began making a name for herself. She played a few exhibitions, too. By her junior year in college, she was the holder of eight titles up and down the Pacific Northwest coast.

Hazel continued her upward spiral, but it didn't mean she was invincible. She had wild days when balls refused to stay in the court, and on occasion a sound, confident baseliner could keep her pinned in the backcourt. In a match this was an awful thing that chipped away at her confidence. Then her quick feet grew reluctant to charge forward and her net game began to melt away. But she never lost composure or concentration.

Chapter 3

MAY SUTTON AND TENNIS TRIUMPHS

THE RIVALRY BETWEEN MAY SUTTON AND HAZEL HOTCHKISS STIRRED UP PLENTY of regional partisanship in California, whose salubrious weather was nearly perfect for tennis year-round. Up and down the coast the two thrilled capacity audiences as they battled for the unofficial title of queen of American women's tennis. U.S. rankings were not established until 1913.

May Sutton was first on the scene. The youngest of five daughters of a British sea captain who had taken his family and moved to the New World to retire in Santa Monica, she had gone east as a seventeen-year-old girl and won the 1904 U.S. Championships. She followed that up with three trips to Wimbledon in 1905, 1906, and 1907, losing only once. This pretty much established her as number one in America, as well as the worldwide queen of tennis. Small as the tennis scene was then, the adulation was still considerable and went straight to her head. She wore the crown as if it was never meant to belong to another.

Since travel was so arduous and time-consuming, and since May Sutton liked things convenient and going her way, unless a tournament paid her expenses she preferred to stay in California most of the time. The world could seek her out in the West.

Hazel was a few months younger and a late starter in tennis by today's standards. She played where her rapidly improving tennis took her, always exhibiting her revolutionary style. She was a born volleyer. In a newspaper article that she wrote analyzing the game then, she attributed her fast learning rate to playing baseball with her brothers. But they had stopped playing tennis with her because she didn't hit the ball hard enough and it bored them.

Speed, Hazel professed, was the backbone of the game. But one had to practice a lot to be accurate, for without accuracy there would be no winning. She learned the fine points of the game by watching other players. The fastest way to improve, she said, was to play with better players, and she complained politely that she didn't have good players to practice with.

Already she was using tactics that are evident at the highest levels of tennis today, especially on slower surfaces. She cleverly chopped the ball low to her opponent's backhand and charged the net behind it, for example. She always tried to put her opponent out of position to set up the crosscourt volley. She had learned these intricacies by watching aggressive men players.

The possibility of a showdown with May Sutton would set any gallery buzzing with anticipation. It was northerner versus southerner, newcomer against the reigning champion. But most of all it was the intrigue of the aggressively quick, angular Hotchkiss volley game against the blistering long drives of Sutton's ground game. Their contrasting personalities fed the flames.

After thirty years of women's pitty-pat play—garden-variety semi-lobs and weedy chops that had grown into harder and harder ground strokes—followers of the game had wondered when, if ever, this monotony would change. They were ecstatic about Hazel Hotchkiss. Her style was cataclysmic. The question was, could it eventually grow strong enough to usurp women's tennis? And would it be an inspiration for future generations? The answer was a qualified yes.

As Hazel gradually branched out from her Bay Area testing fields, the two leading California ladies ended up playing singles against each other probably less than a dozen times, counting exhibitions. Ten matches are documented. They would have preferred falling face down in mud before ten thousand tennis fans to losing a match. And losing to each other was a hundred times worse. They were like pit bulls in lace.

Their relationship fell just short of being an outright personality clash. For the most part, they were civil to each other, politely cool, at times glacial, and on rare occasions bitter, but not overtly ugly. These were women who could stare. Hazel had blue-gray eyes that were steady and unwavering above her strong Roman nose. Her face, not so expressive, was squarish under dark hair she wore in a bun on court as most ladies did. May Sutton had an impassive roundish face under dark blonde curly hair that Hazel envied.

Newspapers and magazines in those florid, wordy times were gentler in their descriptions than they would be now. It was the time of propriety and manners. Then, for example, ladies' ages were never mentioned. If writers were going to jump on something it would be even the smallest irregularity in etiquette or the dress code. A shorter than normal skirt or sleeve could send an audience into an absolute tizzy.

The rivalry was strong enough to last for many years after the smoke of battle had cleared, as Dodo Bundy Cheney, May Sutton's daughter, can attest. Dodo, a legendary senior champion in our modern times with well over three hundred national titles, became very close to Hazel as a young girl learning the game. It was a warm mentor-student relationship that continued later as Dodo Bundy developed into a top ten international player.

Dodo wouldn't always listen to her headstrong, fractious mother. But she would to the thoughtful Hazel, who was willing to go out of her way for the eager child. Small wonder that Hazel won the girl's steadfast affection. "She was like a second mother to me," Dodo Cheney says. "And you know," she adds with a wink, "I think it was another way for her to get back at Mother."

But before the rivalry could develop, Hazel first had to break through the Sutton juggernaut, which dominated women's tennis the length of the Pacific Coast. By 1906 it had already been a joke for a few years that May, Ethel, Violet, and Florence Sutton of Pasadena beat everybody in sight. The prestigious Southern California Championships were humorously referred to as the Sutton California Championships, and at big tournaments and country clubs all the way up to Canada the popular saying of the day was: "It takes a Sutton to beat a Sutton."

May, the youngest, was by far the strongest. Having won Wimbledon the summer of 1905 at eighteen, she was considered the best player in the world. Certainly the All-England Club in 1905 wasn't the teeming showdown site for 128 streamlined professionals that it is now. The collection of amateur ladies looked like they were attending an ice cream social. They were decked out in ankle-length dresses, voluminous petticoats, whalebone corsets under long-sleeved blouses with stiff collars, and large hats, which were finally starting to be discarded as just too bothersome for a serious player.

It was customary for the previous year's winner to sit out the all-comers contest, then face the lone survivor in what was called the challenge round. Between matches on Wimbledon's verdant lawns, and in white tents murmuring with gossip and music and low laughter, servants offered tea, cakes, and strawberries with rich Devonshire cream to dapper aficionados anxious to idolize the next champions.

May Sutton got a lot of attention. The Wimbledon crowd delighted in scrutinizing every inch of the American teenager who had sailed over to see her father's homeland. Their findings were the grist of stadium palaver: the brazen child's uncovered pile of curly blonde hair above that stiff collar she so detested, her rakishly rolled-up blouse sleeves, her unprecedented skirts, which she had shortened by a few inches. Plus she wore fewer petticoats. Such things upset sticky traditionalists.

May was in fact made to lengthen her dress after one of the English competitors objected to seeing the flash of a bare ankle. Only after the correction was made was she allowed on centre court. Ultimately the faux pas were all forgivable because of May's foreign innocence, youth and exuberance.

The whole scene nonetheless constituted a charming, gay milieu. It was as electrically charged by this civilized sporting competition as Strauss's Vienna had been by the waltz. If there was a wistful face among the spectators, it belonged to eighteen-year-old Hazel, who was traveling with a friend and a chaperon, visiting England and Scotland, and playing a lot of "garden tennis." To her "lasting regret" she hadn't entered the tournament. In her diary of the 1905 trip Hazel wrote of the "very nice" conversation with May at Wimbledon. This was before the rivalry between the two developed.

The covetous mother country of lawn tennis claimed to have the world's best tennis for its national championships. After struggling from the first round on, finally beating Dorothea Douglass (Lambert-Chambers) in the first of three consecutive finals they would eventually play, May Sutton agreed. She thought the British women players were superior to the Americans. The evaluation went over well with newspaper reporters and the public, for the stocky, quick-footed, five-foo-four-inch girl was the first foreigner ever to win the ladies singles, as well as the first American to win any title there.

"Magnificently muscular, she appears to care nothing for the minor graces, nor even the little tricks and dodges in which her male compatriots indulge," the *Leicester Chronicle* reported. "She is all for the rigor of the game. There is no tripping after the ball with no showing off her figure at the net. She just stands near the baseline for the most part and sends the ball over the net in terrific drives. Yet, with it all, there is nothing offensively masculine about her. She gives one the impression of being just a fine, healthy, athletic American girl."

May Sutton won Wimbledon in 1905 and again in 1907 and was runner-up in 1906. She made a brief nostalgic appearance in the 1929 draw, losing in the quarters. But in 1905 she had made her first long ocean voyage over with her brother as a vacation to visit her homeland. She had been born in Plymouth before her father moved the family to California.

Possibly revealing the influence that created her formidable forehand, May explained her tennis origins to British writers this way: "Dad's passion for tennis was so great that after he had bought ten acres of land in Pasadena, he made my sisters and me, together with our horse, all pitch in to help him build a court. A short while later the earth embankment collapsed on one side, making it necessary to go slightly uphill in forehand play."

In an earlier attempt in 1904, May Sutton had also won the U.S. Championships. With her extreme western forehand grip, she bedeviled her opponents by imparting far more pace and topspin than they were used to seeing from their normal adversaries using the common eastern and continental grips. They languidly stroked the ball. May Sutton socked it.

"None of us got a set or more than three games from her in the tournament," wrote Elizabeth Moore, the defending champion. "Her California drive took such weird drops and bounds that none of us could handle it. And what seemed still more disconcerting, she would walk into the middle of the court and use that same California forehand with which to volley balls from along the service line." It was a confidence stroke, a vicious roundhouse born of the high bounces off California's hard courts and marked by the free-swinging abandon that characterizes Steffi Graf and Andre Agassi. Moore was baffled by why no eastern girl tried to copy her game, "unless the bounds on grass and wet clay are so low as to discourage the attempt."

Sutton's 1907 Wimbledon victory firmly established her sovereignty as queen of tennis. In October of that year she gave permission for her name to be used on a handsome Wright & Ditson wood racket. "Named after the Lady Champion of the world," the advertising for this leading company proclaimed the "Sutton Star," strung with imported gut, sold for eight dollars and came in three weights up to fifteen ounces. All this was pretty heady stuff for a teenage girl when the vast, jetless planet moved at the pace of the telegraph and locomotive. May Sutton had an attitude. She never thought she should lose to anyone, anywhere, anytime. And she acted it.

Hazel Hotchkiss had to earn her way to the top of the list of Bay Area women players by beating such established local champions as Miriam Edwards and Ethel Ratcliffe, Mary's older sister, who was UC Berkeley's leading player. Twice in three years, Hazel won the State Championships at the Hotel Rafael in San Rafael. But the word "State" seemed hollow, since few Southern Californians came up for it. The Sutton sisters were otherwise occupied.

In September of 1906 the sisters decided to come up for the Pacific Coast Championships at the hotel. May Sutton was now believed to be a mortal after all. She had lost her crown in the finals of Wimbledon earlier in the year. "Local players may wrest laurels from Miss Sutton," one advance story headline dared to suggest. Under it was a picture of Hazel Hotchkiss, the defending champion.

And so it was that on September 6, 1906, the threat of Hazel Hotchkiss became real. She had just beaten Mrs. Ethel (Sutton) Bruce, becoming "the first player outside of the Sutton family to defeat a Sutton in tournament play in some years," the newspapers reported. The victory was significant but the tournament wasn't, since May Sutton defaulted because of illness, and Hazel won the final easily over another Southern California lady, Miss Gabriel Dobbins, considered the best outside of the Suttons.

In the intimate, gracious Rafael Hotel setting, the White Sewing Machine Company gave a social for the finalists after the event, as it had attracted many fashion-conscious motorists. The *San Francisco Examiner* reported the finals had drawn many hotel guests and "pretty girls in their summer frocks, sufficiently escorted by tanned young men in summer flannels."

Beating Ethel Sutton Bruce was important. Hazel had destroyed the Sutton myth. The greater significance, though, was that in singles she had volleyed her way to victory. Women didn't play that way. Only a few men did.

The attacking net style then, as now, was the hallmark of men's doubles. In singles, the ploy took just as much guile but more speed and energy, and of course dexterous, quick hands, to cover twice as much ground. Most of all, it took imagination. The angles and soft shots made it more artful. A net player also had to leap up to smash a ball overhead, or turn and chase one down that got by up there— not exactly a graceful move.

It took courage to play this risky way. It was rushing in for the kill, piling on pressure by forcing a quick resolution to the rally. In doing this, Hazel was just following her instinct for the game. Picking the ball right out of the air and hitting it before it bounced had been the sort of heads-up tennis that had electrified her when she first saw doubles played. Long baseline rallies she had seen earlier had bored her.

Hazel had already won the Pacific Coast Championship and had polished off Elizabeth Ryan of Pasadena 6-4, 6-3 in the finals of the Pacific Northwest in 1907. But in the Pacific States tournament in September, which *American Lawn Tennis* magazine called "the greatest championship ever held on the Pacific slope," Flo Sutton reminded her of just how rugged the House of Sutton was. Hazel was the defending champion and held "every possible title in the North," the papers said, but none of it made Flo flinch. Taking advantage of Hazel's "unsteady" day, Flo won 6-4, 6-3. "[Hazel Hotchkiss] plays in better form than any lady player ever seen on this coast," the magazine said, "but lacks that steady get-back game of Miss Sutton's."

Lack of grit was never a weak point of Hazel's. She won her third State Singles title that same year with a badly bruised left arm that had kept her bedridden for the ten previous days. She got the injury horseback riding when she was thrown off. She never did tell her parents for fear they wouldn't allow her to defend her title. "I never get nervous when I'm playing," she told a local newspaper afterward. "And I generally know how I am going to play before I enter a contest. While I didn't feel exceptionally good, I was quite sure I would win." Because of her unpretentious poise and sincerity, her remarks never sounded conceited.

Meanwhile, during that summer of 1907, perky May Sutton had returned finally from her Wimbledon triumph. Stopping at Niagara on the Lake in Canada, "the world's champion drew great crowds of spectators" at the Queen's Royal Courts in racing through the ladies' singles with the loss of only three games. Moving on to Cincinnati, she won the Tri-State for the third time. "If she [May Sutton] plays at all next season it is likely to be only in California where she has been practically missing for the past three seasons on account of her trips abroad," *American Lawn Tennis* said. "Miss Sutton won the state women's championship when she was barely thirteen years old." May was just turning twenty-one then, a fact hard to find in any tennis reportage. Ladies' ages were so confidential, to mention them in conversation or print was a breach of etiquette.

Hazel entered UC Berkeley in the fall of 1907 at age twenty and became a language student, choosing German because French was too hard for her to pronounce. She lived six months out of the year in the Kappa Kappa Gamma sorority house, although she preferred living at home. Her sorority sisters, impressed with her efficiency as a go-getter and quiet leadership qualities as much as her fame as a tennis player, elected her president. Living in helped her keep better track of sorority matters. Despite a busy schedule, she was active on the *Blue and Gold* yearbook staff and, as campus women's tennis champion, organized a women's team to play matches against Stanford, the forerunner of varsity women's intercollegiate tennis. She had to teach some of the girls how to play.

She quickly found that a lack of good practice during school could ruin her in a tournament. Golda Meyer kept her from a third consecutive Bay Counties title in October, and in February of 1908, Flo Sutton, fighting off a match point, beat her in an unusual semifinal match down south in the Coronado Country Club's big annual tournament on the beach. Homer, who was to lose in the men's consolation singles final, had taken his sister down on the train, as all women in those days traveled with a chaperon or companion.

The semifinalists lined up like California all-stars: Hazel, Flo, Mrs. R. D. Farquhar (Marion Jones), and Mrs. B. O. Bruce (Ethel Sutton). May Sutton was the sit-out champion. Officially, Flo beat Hazel 10-8, 5-7, 6-3 over two days. Hazel had held, and lost, a match point in the third before the games had gone to 6-all when the match was called on account of darkness. The next day, officials ordered that they start a new set altogether. So it took fifty-one games to settle the three-setter. In the championship round baby sister May drubbed Flo "mercilessly," *American Lawn Tennis* magazine reported, 6-1, 6-2.

Still, by the summer of 1908 Hazel held no less than four California State singles championships, a roomful of trophies, and a big reputation as Northern California's best. That summer her father let her play six to eight weeks of the Pacific Northwest tennis circuit, the first of three summers she would do this. She stayed with families who were members of the posh clubs hosting the tournaments. They warmly welcomed the clever, diminutive girl with the man-sized net tactics. Hazel made lasting friendships and looked forward to returning each year to repeat her successes.

Hazel Hotchkiss was not an overpowering player. Her serve was not fast, or complicated with spin, but was well placed. Her ground strokes were chopped and neutralizing, not menacing like May Sutton's forehand. In a tight spot, she could put a well-disguised lob on a dime. In order to go to the net herself, she waited for the short ball before advancing on in behind it. Then, as one newspaper reported, "she went up in the air to volley the ball like a fox terrier after a butterfly." For a woman to have any overhead at all was a rarity. Hers was athletic and extremely accurate. In his book *Match Play and the Spin of the Ball*, Bill Tilden called her "the greatest of all women net players" and said "the perfect game for a woman" would have to include her overhead and volley.

As much as any player before or after, Hazel used her head to discern weaknesses. Once she won a match easily that everyone predicted she'd be lucky to struggle through. "I didn't give her a shot she liked to hit," she explained. Another time she played a girl at least a half foot taller who had a ferocious serve. Hazel was told she wouldn't be able to return it. "Well," she recalled later in *American Heritage*, "I said I'm going to have my racket flat and hit the ball in the middle and get it back, and if she is not used to people getting the ball back, she won't be ready for the return. That was my psychology. So after I got her serve back, she was so surprised she didn't return the shot. It wasn't that I was smart or brilliant or had beautiful shots, but I kept myself from getting caught."

That was Hazel Hotchkiss—analytic but simple, direct, and self-effacing. These qualities, which smacked of a rural or perhaps frontier upbringing, endeared her to more generations of tennis players than anyone in history, man or woman. Her innocence and forthrightness, coming from so small a figure, tended to cut through like a clear note in a recital hall.

Invariably, when Hazel played singles exhibitions against men, newspapers would never fail to mention her diminutive size and then compare in detail her strengths and weaknesses to what men could accomplish. Today it sounds laughably sexist. "This slip of a girl plays tennis like a strong man" was the headline of a Portland newspaper over an August 20, 1907 story about her exhibition with Brandt Wickersham, the Irvington Club's leading player. It began: "A slip of a girl with tiny hands and feet, just a shade under five dozen inches in height and barely out of her teens—such is Miss Hazel Hotchkiss of Berkeley, California, who despite her distinctly feminine appearance, demonstrated to a crowd of delighted tennis enthusiasts yesterday that it is not beyond the power of a woman to master the difficult strokes essayed by the highest class of male experts of the racket."

They split sets, incidentally, and "Wick never loafed nor dubbed."

A major influence in the maturing of Hazel's game was Maurice McLoughlin, an explosive, well-liked player of heroic dimension. He practically tore the cover off the ball serving cannonballs and huge twists, racing to attack every ball, gain the net, smash the putaway. A good-natured youth with humble origins, he had learned the game and created the style on the public courts of Golden Gate Park. When he got good enough, the California Tennis Association paid his way east and he became the first man to bring the ultimately aggressive, western hard-court style to the delicate eastern grass. He revolutionized the men's game. Dazzled East Coast reporters had dubbed the six-foot-tall redhead "The California Comet." When McLoughlin stepped onto the turf, Bill Tilden wrote in *Match Play and the Spin of the Ball*, "the god Speed was at the wheel." McLoughlin became the world's number one player in 1912, the year his doubles partner, Tom Bundy of Los Angeles, married May Sutton.

Hazel's relationship with McLoughlin in workouts and mixed doubles events was one of the most enjoyable of her playing career. "A more unselfish friend or more inspiring partner would be hard to imagine," she wrote. "He was always willing to come over from San Francisco and play on our court. . . . He was then perfecting his marvelous smash, one of the most effective and beautiful kills in tennis history. Of course I benefited in many ways and improved my game much sooner than I should have done otherwise. I was proud to be his partner, and the desire to continue to be good enough was a great spur to my ambition."

McLoughlin once offered to teach Hazel his beautiful, arched-back twist serve. In those days the feet had to stay behind the baseline until the delivery motion was completed. McLoughlin kicked his right leg up a little for more power but without ever letting it cross the plane of the baseline. It was a very physical serve. "But I told him, 'I'm not built that way,'" she told an interviewer. "'I have short arms, short legs, and it isn't comfortable to throw the ball the way you want me to do it.' I suppose I was too feminine, but I couldn't do a serve that would put me off balance. All I could think of was to keep my short, square body on balance."

With Hazel's growing status it only followed that about then she would be invited to play an exhibition against a man. She had nothing against it. That's the way she had grown up competing, against men.

"People always wanted to see how good I would be against a man," she wrote. "To their delight I usually won. The gallery seemed to be always with me, and the man so polite that he never played his best until I had quite a lead, which is what often happens in mixed singles. The man tries to exchange shots and does not feel called on to play his best game, usually a smashing game from the back court or the net, while the woman is playing the type of game at which she excels. I played the leading men players at that time, but in the twenty years since, except for Helen Wills, I have rarely heard of a woman playing in an exhibition match against a man."

In the fall of 1908, a quartet of eastern men came to California to play in the Pacific Coast Championships, and also to recruit more western entries for the national championships back east. They were duly impressed with Hazel's game, and one of them, Wallace F. Johnson, persuaded her mother, Emma, to consent to sending her to Philadelphia the next summer. So the next season, 1909, after first defending her Oregon State and Washington State singles titles, she and her father, W. J., traveled five days by train to the imposing Philadelphia Cricket Club, where the U.S. Championships for ladies were contested on grass. Hazel, who had just completed her sophomore year, passed the hours on the train by cross-stitching designs on six towels she was making into Christmas presents.

Hazel had only seen a few grass courts in the Pacific Northwest. At the stately columned Cricket Club she was awed by a vast contiguous number of them, like an emerald sea divided by waves of black nets topped with their pert white tapes. But it rained every day. When the courts were playable they were still slippery as ice for the crude high-top black sneakers that the women wore. "Hideous things," Hazel called them.

All her matches were easy until the all-comers finals, when she needed three sets to beat Louise Hammond of New York. In the championship round, playing in a sleeveless dimity dress, she brushed aside Maud Barger-Wallach of Newport and New York, a delicate woman who was thirty-nine and served underhanded. She was about the only one left from the old crowd who did. Maud had given up a career as an artist after falling in love with tennis at age thirty and becoming devoted to it. But Hazel Hotchkiss was a new breed of player and in a class of her own.

To Hazel, whose youthful speed and ball anticipation were so apparent, Mrs. Barger-Wallach appeared to be old and thin, reminding Hazel of her grandmother. *The New Yorker*, recounting the 1909 championship singles match in 1952 with some imagination, said that Mrs. Barger-Wallach sported "a wide-brimmed garden hat and a flowing white gown that gave her the appearance of a displaced Renoir."

"She wore black stockings and had long sleeves and a skinny little figure," Hazel said. Having been ill for some time, Mrs. Barger-Wallach had searched her conscience before the match over whether to default. She decided finally that facing the match with courage was preferable.

Perhaps after the first set she had second thoughts, for Hazel swept it in ten minutes with the loss of a scant six points. Then Hazel began the second set in the same ruthless fashion. But before she was halfway through, she ceased playing to Mrs. Barger-Wallach's weak backhand and began to hit to her forehand. Some beautiful points ensued.

The audience warmed to the display. And Mrs. Barger-Wallach, even losing the last set 6-1, looked like a creditable, graceful player after all.

"I don't think that Hazel's courtesy toward Mrs. Barger-Wallach was lost on many of us who saw her on that first trip east," a USLTA official who had seen the match told *The New Yorker* magazine more than forty years later. However, it was Hazel's overhead smash that drew the most commentary throughout the tournament.

"Remember," the official reminisced, "none of us had ever seen a girl who could smash or volley like a man. Until Hazel came along, you know, mixed doubles was quite an ordeal for the female half of the team. The men ungallantly directed their fire at the female on the opposing team whenever they needed to clinch an important point and took all the putaway shots. A number of players took everything. Hazel restored a balance to mixed doubles. It was very enjoyable, I must admit, watching this unassuming girl from California smashing the ball plumb at the feet of our celebrated court-hogs."

The same afternoon Hazel returned to the court to win the women's doubles with Edith Rotch of Boston, then the mixed doubles with Wallace Johnson, the man who had persuaded her mother to let her make the trip.

Hazel wasn't a fashion plate and considered herself rather plain-looking. To an audience, because of her diminutive size and her quick style and cleverness, she must have seemed charming. She wore white dimity dresses her mother made for her that extended to within four inches of the ground. A corset kept her stockings up. The dresses were of thin cotton, usually corded or checked, full, stiff, and with a round neck. The daring short sleeves freed her arms to make crisp overheads and volleys.

Hazel liked the dresses but always felt they would have looked so much better on someone who was "more feminine-looking." She wore her long hair, which she regarded as being of poor quality, in a bun. To keep it from sliding down her neck she wore a ribbon tied around it in a bow. She thought that looked silly, if not horrible. Sometimes she wore a bandeau, a tennis style that would become the trend, replacing hats. It didn't matter that she wasn't a fashion plate, she said, because she saw herself as having a square body, "like a horse," implying that beautiful clothes would be wasted on her. She was happy to let her tennis make her statement and to be recognized for it.

May Sutton was different. "She had a lovely figure," Hazel said. "She had blonde curly hair—I'd give anything to have curls—oh, she was a lovely-looking person . . . and the stamina of a horse, strong and determined."

But the queen was nowhere to be found around Philadelphia again for the fifth straight year. May Sutton never did return, in fact, after winning so easily there in 1904. Often people couldn't make sense out of her decisions. She was so fiercely independent that her priorities seemed jumbled and incoherent. For example, in October of 1909, three months after Hazel became national champion, May showed up in the East to win the Niagara on the

Lake and Western tournaments in New York. On the train ride home she stopped off in Cleveland to play an exhibition against the men's city champion, H. F. Pettie, which she won 6-3, 7-9, 6-4. More than likely though, in a family of nine (five girls, two boys), just where May Sutton played depended first on whether a tournament paid some or all of her expenses and second on her whim. England had apparently been anxious for her, and generous.

American women's tennis now was thoroughly dominated by Californians, grass courts posing no mystery or obstacle to the westerners. "Miss Hotchkiss is the greatest woman player ever to play here [in Philadelphia], with the possible exception of Miss May Sutton," the *New York Times* reported, pointing out, too, that Hazel's triple crown sweep was a feat unequaled by May Sutton. Still, Hazel hadn't yet played May Sutton in singles, and despite all her accolades, she was not immune to the other Sutton sisters. Florence especially was always eager to tarnish Hazel's crown.

When Hazel and May did confront each other on the court it was anticlimactic because May Sutton won so convincingly. Hazel did not have a big shot from the baseline. She could only attack off a return that fell short. Then she would chop her approach shot deep into a corner and start for the net. Her legs weren't long enough to take her quickly in close so she could comfortably volley away the return. Often she was caught at mid-court on the service line digging out low volleys. But this was a great strength of hers. Bill Tilden said Hazel had the best half-volley of all time among women. It always drew a crowd's attention because no woman could perform there in that awful, vulnerable no-man's-land like she could. Then, after making a laudable offensive shot from this defensive position, Hazel came the rest of the way in to the net and angled away the next return—an attempted pass or lob—for a winner.

May Sutton's forehand didn't permit the pattern, however. Running around her backhand as often as possible, May's forehands, struck low to the ground, were hard and deep into the corners, delivering a dipping ball spinning so fast it almost buzzed, accurate practically to the inch, and as difficult to control after its exploding bounce as a runaway horse. As soon as Hazel threatened with an approach shot, zip, the passing shot flew past her.

In their first meeting Hazel got five games in two sets. May's forehand blew her off the court. It must have been bewildering. In all Hazel's mounting tournament experience, East, Pacific Northwest, and Bay Area, she had never faced such power from a woman.

Gradually the college girl who had a penchant for analyzing things that needed it, and leaving alone things that didn't, began to win more games. She mixed her shots better. She found a "tell" in May's forehand preparation that helped her anticipate May's target. And she began obsessively picking on May's defensively chopped backhand.

Hazel also stopped viewing May's swaggering as impudent effrontery, especially after being passed at the net with scorching forehands. Cool equanimity was the antidote for that. Hazel used to say that the way May beat her sisters was she made them mad first.

When at last Hazel won a set from May Sutton the second week in February 1910, she became the only American female to do so outside of the Sutton family. It was at the Coronado Country Club in San Diego County. Again there was the murmuring, expectant gallery. To lose a set in front of it was tantamount to a slap in the face for the snobbish May Sutton, the prima donna who always got her way.

Following an intermission after they had each won 6-3 sets, the players were "grim with determination" according to the nation's leading tennis magazine. At 4-all in the third, May's ground strokes found the lines on the big points in "hot and fierce" games, and she closed the match 6-4.

Ten days later, Hazel played through to the final at a tournament held at the Hotel Virginia in Long Beach. May, wanting to demoralize the pesky contender, got revenge with a sweet 6-2, 6-3 thumping in front of a crowd of two thousand, "again proving her superiority," the newspapers said. Hazel had to be content with her semifinal trouncing of Florence, then winning the mixed with Maurice McLoughlin, with whom she had also won the Coronado event.

A Hazel-May exhibition match that year, which May won, drew three thousand spectators. Meanwhile, women's tennis elsewhere suffered the absence of these two. *American Lawn Tennis* magazine pointed out at this time that the Women's Indoor Nationals in New York had "an entry list decidedly lacking in class," a class May and Hazel had created.

The rivalry gathered steam. A few months later, in the spring of 1910, the tables finally turned, and the House of Sutton lay momentarily in shambles. It was at the famous Ojai Valley tournament at Nordhoff. Scores of volunteers put together a large, colorful, all-inclusive event that has survived to this day. Then it was played on dirt (technically clay) and was a major Southern California event with global significance. The Sutton-Hotchkiss rivalry added a spice that stretched the event's dimensions to a nonpareil sectional feud. They were both twenty-three. May's famous Sutton Star tennis racket, with the star below the slotted throat, was, with the best lamb's gut, selling briskly among ladies nationwide for around eight dollars. The handle was typically five inches around, gargantuan to modern thinking. But that was the size men and women alike used, and so did Hazel.

Ojai was not just a tournament. It was a state of mind. Perfection, grace, style. Here is how *American Lawn Tennis* magazine rhapsodically described it in a brief account of Hazel's 2-6, 6-4, 6-0 historic win:

"The sensational victory was hard for the throng that crowded in the grandstand to realize that the impossible was actually occurring before their eyes. It was perfect tournament conditions in a setting of live oaks, rugged mountains nearby and dense treetop foliage close by. . . . It was a sunlit sward dotted with gay sunshades and enlivened by casual strolling groups of white-skirted athletic girls and stalwart flannel-clad youths . . . a picture long to be remembered. A commodious and artistic grandstand built last year added greatly to the comfort of the spectators and was made a thing of beauty by the masses of flowers in the club colors—blue brodiaca and yellow poppies and mustard—with which it was tastefully decorated. Pennants and banners of two score or more schools and colleges usually represented in the entry list waved here and there, giving an added touch of color to the scene."

Tea and ices and rolls, salad, and coffee were served in the piazza of the pretty little clubhouse under the oaks. Even the courts were new. They were likened to a "billiard table with no shade and ample room at the sides and ends." This was the marriage of West Coast tennis and American gentility in a style and atmosphere never to be matched again.

May Sutton, who had been Pasadena's Rose Queen in 1908 and off court dressed with a flair for pearls, silk, lace, and feather boas, did not shake hands after the match. As one woman who knew her said: "No one was quite good enough for May. She was belligerent about being the best." This attitude worked a hardship on everyone, even May's husband. Years later, Hazel described it bluntly in an interview with *American Heritage* magazine, as if old wounds had opened just remembering those days. "She was very hard for me to play against because she was not ladylike—she was rude, she was unsportsmanlike—and it upset me.

"With May Sutton it's awfully hard for me to criticize her at all because she didn't know any better. She was the youngest of four girls (excluding Adele, the non-playing sister) and she beat them all. And she beat them because she could make them mad. It wasn't necessary, because she could have outplayed them by using her head. She didn't have the head—I'm not criticizing her, but she wouldn't go to school. She no more could have analyzed a shot than a cow."

Hazel envied May's curly hair and figure, her strength and steely determination. But May's spoiled behavior, even by today's loose standards and with a public craving zany incidents, would have raised hackles. It started with the warm-up.

"She didn't give me a ball [to hit]," Hazel said. "If I picked the ball off the ground and knocked it to her—ordinary players knock it back and forth—she knocked it out of reach. She didn't let me hit a ball. I don't think she knew what she was doing. My idea of tennis was to give the other person a chance to practice, but as I got smarter and thought about it, I realized it might be good for me to keep the ball away from her, too. But I couldn't do that. That's not the way it should be.

"The umpire told her, 'Miss Sutton, you are not supposed to delay the game.' She said, 'If you don't like the way I play, I won't play any more.' Imagine. Imagine!"

In 1912 May married Tom Bundy, a very fine and popular Los Angeles player who was McLoughlin's doubles partner and a friend of many players north and south, including Hazel. Hazel said at times Bundy told her he wished Hazel would beat the socks off his wife.

"He [Tom Bundy] said two different times when I played her, he said, 'Hazel, I hope you win today. You deserve to win. You're an awfully good player and May needs a lesson.'"

There's no indication that May learned anything from her 1910 defeat at Nordhoff. When she lost the last point she was at the service line and just walked directly off the court. Hazel had to run around the net post and chase her down to shake hands. "Well, May, I was lucky today," Hazel remembered saying, to which May Sutton said nothing and kept walking.

Of course, May's effrontery on that day at Nordhoff remained an often-told anecdote in the ensuing months as the tennis crowd asked: Is the Sutton reign over?

The bulk of 1910 turned out to be a fabulous season for Hazel Hotchkiss. She repeated the hat trick at the women's U.S. Championships in Philadelphia, which May ignored as usual. As was customary until the rules were changed in 1919, Hazel, as defending champion, sat out the singles until the draw offered her a finals opponent. Among other tournaments she won that year were the California State and the Washington State, where she added a footnote to her growing reputation. According to *American Lawn Tennis* magazine, she defeated a Miss Huiskamp of Seattle in the semifinals without the loss of a single point. *American Lawn Tennis* magazine was impressed further by the fact that Huiskamp had advanced from the quarters by a 6-0, 6-0 score herself.

It was six months of rampant speculation before the question of who was number one was answered. It came in a hard-fought final of the Pacific Coast Championship at Del Monte. Playing the power game, and invariably running around her backhand, May won the first set 7-5. Hazel, displaying a contrasting style of touch volleys and beautifully placed overhead smashes, took the second 6-4 and then went to the baseline to continue with the deciding set. But May had vacated the court. Moreover, she had walked over to inform the umpire she would rather like to have some hot tea. Then she sat herself down in a wicker chair and waited in silence for a hotel waiter to serve her on a tray.

By most accounts, twenty minutes passed before May was ready to resume play. She then pulled out the match 6-4 in the third. We will never know just how deeply Hazel stewed. May Sutton knew exactly what she was doing with this shenanigan and knew she could get away with it. Typically, though, there was an optional ten-minute rest for women after split sets.

The effect on the gallery was predictable. The southerners thought May's ploy was a gambit acceptable within the rules, or a slightly stretched version of them. Indeed, it was creative underhandedness: a queen did deserve her tea. But the northerners weren't buying it. They thought it was bad sportsmanship, period. The match only fueled interest in the rivalry. The edge May held had never been thinner. What would happen next?

In other events that year, Hazel had been busy solidifying her reputation in the East. Again she had gone to the U.S. Championships in Philadelphia. Again she repeated the hat trick, and without the loss of a single set. As defending champion, she didn't have to play a singles match until the draw offered her Louise Hammond of New York, whom she defeated 6-4, 6-2.

The next year, 1911, was probably the height of Hazel's playing career, although she continued to achieve various high distinctions over the ensuing years. In the spring, at age twenty-four, she graduated from UC Berkeley as a member of Prytanean, the University's honor society for women students. This delighted her father, who had dutifully traveled east with her for the women's nationals each of the two previous summers and had been a hit of sorts in tennis circles himself. According to one eastern sports writer's account, Mr. Hotchkiss was a pleasant, unassuming man, "most entertaining and companionable, and, best and rarest of all, not inclined to lug 'my daughter' into the conversation every other minute." The commencement present he gave her was not just the trip east but also his permission for her to remain in theEast for the first time to play the circuit after the U.S. Championships in Philadelphia. It was probably the most tennis she had ever played at one time.

By today's standards, of course, players then did not work hard on their games at all. They were amateurs and played only in season. Most didn't particularly have much endurance, Hazel included. "I didn't know what it was to go 'into training,'" Hazel said. "I didn't practice. I played probably once or twice a week. That was all the chance I had. I played with one of my brothers or a boyfriend."

The result of playing one tournament week after another for four months was that Hazel cleaned up. According to one count, she won two dozen trophies (ten singles and the rest doubles and mixed) as she went undefeated from mid-July to mid-October. She returned home with plenty of memories this time. An especially rich one was of a certain young Harvard man, George Wightman.

Hazel had started her 1911 winning streak by establishing a record at Philadelphia that most thought would stand for several decades. She won a third straight triple sweep. Her closest match of the entire eastern experience was the finals. She beat Flo Sutton 8 10, 6 1, 9 7. The match had started under a threatening storm. Here's the way *American Lawn Tennis* described the atmosphere:

"The challenge match was begun shortly before 3 P.M. on Saturday with by far the largest crowd of the week in attendance. The championship court was surrounded by several rows of spectators, while the spacious porch of the club fronting the court was packed to its utmost capacity. The two sturdy young ladies from sunny California fairly radiated health, looking fit for the most grueling of battles. To the majority of the spectators it seemed a foregone conclusion that Miss Hotchkiss would retain her title, although a fairly close match was expected, but the titanic struggle that ensued exceeded the dreams of the most imaginative. Towards the close of the final set the tension which held the throng almost reached the limit of human endurance, and with few exceptions the nerve-racked spectators emitted long-drawn sighs of relief when the deciding point was scored."

Aggressively, Hazel had jumped to a 4-1 first set lead, only to tighten up when Flo Sutton came back to tie it up. It was a seesaw to 8-all. Then Flo broke through to take the marathon set and grabbed a 1-0 lead. That was a wake-up call for Hazel. With all of her shots suddenly working, and thoughtfully mixed, she won six straight for the second set. After a seven-minute rest, however, Flo Sutton came out hitting the ball much harder than at any time during the tournament, and with accuracy. She was even bold enough to surprise Hazel by stealing the net away a few times. Hazel lost some confidence. Her overheads got soft and some flew wild. But even playing cautiously she managed to stay even. Down match point at 6-5, 40-30, Hazel came up with a clutch overhead winner off a deep lob. At 7-all Hazel apparently put up a "superhuman effort" to surge ahead and win her third title in a row with a winning volley.

Next, playing a starring role and showing no ill effects from the marathon, Hazel dazzled the gallery with volleys and overheads in winning the mixed doubles—where again the men insisted on pounding the ball at the ladies—and the women's doubles. The latter was interrupted by rain, the match resuming on a slick court that at times had all four players falling down and bouncing back up to stay in the three-setter's crucial points. Hazel ended the last match at 7:42 P.M., having played a total of eight sets lasting eighty-nine games.

The surprise of the season was the appearance in early September of May Sutton. She came to a popular tournament in a beautiful spot in upstate New York. The event was Niagara on the Lake, which May had won in 1909.

It was the first time May and Hazel had met outside of California and the first time they had faced each other on a grass court. In the final, light precipitation bedeviled the court after May had annexed the first set 6-0. May jumped to a 5-1 lead in the second. At some point the umpire had given the players the option to don spikes. May huffily refused the offer. "I don't need spikes," she said, as if a switch was demeaning. But Hazel thought spikes might stabilize her and be a safeguard against playing any worse. Putting on the lightweight black leather shoes with the penny nails through the soles set her wheels going, literally and figuratively. Hazel vowed to capitalize on the slippery court conditions and run May more, plus hit behind her at the right times. Facing the fact she had lost eleven of twelve games didn't faze her at all.

She later wrote in *Better Tennis*, "On the verge of defeat . . . I suddenly said to myself 'That's no lead'—a phrase which has been long familiar to everyone I teach—and began to use my head. I realized that I was not getting down low enough to hit the balls in a way to lift them up, for the court was very wet. It was soggy when we began and kept getting worse because of the drizzle. As I steadied down I gained confidence and came through triumphant—in time to go to Newport to see Maurice McLoughlin play in the finals of the Men's National. . . . ."

Hazel's confidence allowed her to eke out the second set 7-5 and then humiliate the dispirited May Sutton 6-0 in the third, a memory May wished to forget but no doubt took to the grave. Imagine, winning twelve straight games from May Sutton. It would be an oft-told story, coast to coast.

"When I won she [May] started to walk off the court just the way she had before," Hazel told *American Heritage*. "Then as I walked up to the stadium she said something like 'stinkpot tennis!' She was describing the game I had played. It meant nothing to me especially, except I remembered it."

This isolated result certainly wasn't enough for anyone to make a claim that Hazel was the better player in the scheme of history. But it proved that Hazel was always a danger to May, where before no one was. May had the record on her side. In the period since Hazel had won the 1909 championships up to that time in September 1911 (some twenty-seven months), the two women had played each other eight times and May had prevailed in six. Three of those were close and three were lopsided wins by May. One was an exhibition. Hazel's two wins were three-setters.

The two ladies played twice more; May won one and Hazel, many years later in 1928, when they were forty-one, won the second. It was at the U.S. Championships at Forest Hills. In a wonderfully nostalgic nail-biter, Hazel won 6-4, 11-9. She went on to reach the quarterfinals in her last appearance in the singles draw but took the women's doubles title with Helen Wills. The lifetime record: three for Hazel, seven for May.

In 1912, both of them got married and began different lifestyles. Hazel's was destined to become a quite active matronly role in tennis that affected practically every American female star for fifty years. The famous Sutton-Hotchkiss clashes became the high-water mark on the dam of California tennis history, a passel of fond stories told by chatty women and dapper old men, full of color and signifying the state's passion for the game.

Herbert Warren Wind of *The New Yorker* assessed it this way: "In this strong and colorful rivalry, which continued without diminution of ardor until 1912, when Hazel Hotchkiss married and moved east, the real winner was California. Hitherto the state had exhibited a patchy and rather casual concern for tennis, but the dramatic overtones of the Hotchkiss-Sutton series created in both the upper and lower sectors of the state a profound tennis-consciousness that California has never lost."

Chapter 4

MARRIAGE, TALENT SCOUTING, AND HELEN WILLS

Hazel had been over-tennised when she got home from her triumphs, tired yet suffused with adrenaline, and giddy from her winning streak and its gratifying acclaim. At such a time, no player really wants to stop for fear the high level can never again be attained. So she consented to play one more event in San Francisco. Besides, she couldn't resist challenges any more than she could sit idly around and do nothing—her hands were always busy. At the tournament, Hazel's first vanquished opponent—embarrassed that she had scored only one game—rather childishly begged her not to let any of her other opponents get more than one game. Hazel consented. The pot thus sweetened, she accomplished this, giving new meaning to the word "focus." "And it demonstrated to me for good the advantage of having a definite objective," she said. Hazel had a knack for finding lessons in her challenges, win or lose.

Meanwhile, her personal life had reached a new, dizzying plateau. "My recent acquaintance, George Wightman . . . had an objective which brought him out of Harvard, graduating in February instead of June, and out to the West Coast," she wrote in her book.

George Wightman was a slim Harvard man who glittered when he walked. He was a fine yachtsman and captain of the varsity tennis team, although he might have been more adept at court tennis. He and his father were also members of the Longwood Cricket Club, one of the first sites used in the formation of lawn tennis in America.

George's father had been a lieutenant of steel baron Andrew Carnegie's, and he had retired young and rich. The Wightmans lived in Brookline in a fabulous, multi-columned mansion, accessible by a circular driveway. Inside, beyond the foyer, a vast, sprawling marble stairway spread up to a capacious landing on the second floor, where its massive banisters veered off on either side to the wings. There on the landing, one of the city's finest pipe organs resided. And there, as a young man, the precocious E. Power Biggs, after obtaining permission, came regularly to practice.

The Wightmans were a family that had all the symbols of wealth and position. On the sunken dirt court behind the mansion, they hosted little one-day round robin tournaments in the summer. As a keen spectator of championship tennis, George had spent the summer before his senior year at Harvard, 1911, observing at many of the best tournaments. At one of these events he saw Hazel and found the young star player very intriguing. They met, and before she returned to the Bay Area he had developed more than a passing fancy for her.

Wightman came out with his family so both clans could look each other over. After a week, Hazel's mother consented to the engagement of the young couple. They were married on February 24, 1912, at the Hotchkiss home on Claremont Avenue. Miller Hotchkiss stood in as best man for the groom. Afterwards, Hazel went back east with the Wightman family to set up home and begin a semi-retirement from active tennis.

The marriage put together a prominent Boston family and a successful, entrepreneurial family of pioneer stock that had crossed the prairie by wagon train. Although the stereotypical images of westerners with extravagant grizzly-bear beards were fading, the East still viewed the West as raw and untamed. A Pony Express route did still exist near Mendocino, above Healdsburg. However, silent movies were being produced, and the invention of the airplane was just starting to catch on. Experimental television broadcasts were twenty long years down the road.

Even though Hazel had brought unprecedented attention to women's tennis in the West and had, as a player, completely won over the East, she had married into strait-laced Boston society, where such a reputation raised eyebrows. This was a realm of afternoon teas, bridge, and volunteer work, and no tricky net game could conquer it.

Boston bluebloods were asking who this Hazel Hotchkiss Wightman was, this tennis player, and where on earth she came from. Just as important, what was her pedigree? It was common in some finicky circles to think of women who played at any sport, and perspired publicly, to be no better than actresses or burlesque queens. In truth, the concept of women as amateur athletes was in its infancy. In the 1912 Olympics, for example, the only women to compete did so in tennis, archery, and figure skating.

Hazel's marriage and entry into Boston society signaled a radical change of lifestyle for her. It was the end of the Hazel Hotchkiss "playing era" and the beginning of the Hazel Wightman epoch. The western girl was to become an eastern lady, a Boston dame in the classic sense of the word, but with portfolio. In it were tennis rackets, scores of them, that later grew to be thousands.

Hazel pared back active participation in tennis and became a mother. She began carving out a diverse personal agenda that was destined to bring her more fame than she had received as a mere player. She became the link between the East and the West Coasts for women in tennis.

As she swelled with her first child, she and her twenty-one-year-old husband lived in the Wightman family mansion in Brookline. Their tennis club was the Longwood Cricket Club in Chestnut Hill. Its finely manicured grass courts were considered by many the tennis center of the nation. Founded in 1877, the club converted all its cricket players to tennis. It was a favorite playing venue of Harvard players, and the first Davis Cup match had been held there in 1900.

Hazel could have had an easy life and rested on her laurels. In its wedding story, February 25, 1912, the *San Francisco Chronicle* described her groom as "one of the wealthiest capitalists in Brookline." That was actually her father-in-law, the steel executive who retired in 1899 at the age of forty-four to build a fabulous mansion for his family. But Hazel was a doer, a compulsive busy bee, and closer in her temperament to populist values and habits. Tennis was for all the people, in her opinion. This was a very "western" thought, promoted, for example, by the deeds of John McLaren, the Golden Gate Park chief who, before the century turned, designed the public park's major tennis complex.

Hazel saw deeply into tennis, saw the backbone it had, and knew intuitively that it could empower the individual with identity and self-esteem. It was a tool for life, to be used by ordinary players and stars alike. This propelling vision was certainly worth building a purpose in life around in a time when the major part of the work women did was domestic, as homemakers or volunteers. So regardless of her condition as an expectant mother, regardless of her new social responsibilities, there was never a doubt that tennis would remain a prime focus for her lifetime. She would be an ambassador of the sport. Exactly how she would apply herself was yet to be determined—that would evolve naturally.

"My tennis playing days were over for a time," she wrote of that first year in Boston. "There were tournaments that summer at Newport and New York, of course, and we attended, and there was plenty of tennis at Longwood, but I followed it all from a chair. My son George was born the following winter."

The happy December event in the Wightman home (at that time babies were customarily born at home) happened, by chance, the day after May Sutton married Tom Bundy at Christ Church in Los Angeles. *American Lawn Tennis* magazine hailed their nuptials as the first in history between champions of this caliber. If the two female rivals were still competing now in the game of life, however, Hazel had an insurmountable lead.

Young George wasn't a year old when Hazel dusted off her rackets and went to the Longwood tournament with a fervent desire to show that mothers could compete, too. There, in September 1913—astonishingly—she defeated her successor, Mary K. Browne, the national champion. Browne had won the U.S. ladies' singles championship at Philadelphia in 1912 and, just as Hazel had done, added both doubles titles. She repeated this "triple" win that people thought was so special for the second time the very month before playing Hazel. It's likely Browne was at the height of her career, too, since she won the triple again in 1914, thus mocking the pundits by equaling the impossible triple-triple that Hazel had accomplished. Leave it to tennis to show Gibraltar is made of clay.

Hazel took one more title that year at Longwood, the mixed doubles. Her partner? Husband George, then in Harvard Law School. Lawn tennis, though, was probably George's third best sport, behind court tennis and sailing. As a teenager he had gained a reputation in several races off the resort town of Hull by outsailing Charles Francis Adams, and he knew the bay waters like a book. All his life, Wightman remained a highly respected yachtsman in bay racing circles and had the enviable record of winning more races than he lost. But according to one sailing columnist who wrote an obituary several decades later, Wightman insisted on having fun, too, and, as a lover of music, even had a piano installed in a thirty-eight-foot motor boat he bought after his sailing days were over.

Hankering to keep her skills sharp on the grindstone of top competition, Hazel went back to Philadelphia to compete in the U.S. Championships quicker than she thought she might. Her first daughter, Virginia, was born in July 1914. The next year, after fighting off a troublesome sprained ankle and a bout of diphtheria, Hazel still managed to play several tournaments. The records show she only lost one singles match that year. It occurred when she volleyed her way into the 1915 National Women's Championships finals. It looked like she might win, too. She was leading one set to love against Molla Bjurstedt, a strong young Norwegian girl. But Hazel simply didn't have the stamina and folded 4-6, 6-2, 6-0. Bjurstedt went on to win three more U.S. women's championships, then four more as Molla Mallory, after marrying an American industrialist. She still holds the record for the most women's singles titles: eight. As it turned out, in 1915 Hazel had been only a set away from performing the triple-win hat trick a fourth time, for she went on in the tournament to win the women's doubles and the mixed.

Little is known about Hazel's on-again, off-again tennis career in the years between 1915 and 1919. Another daughter, Hazel Hotchkiss Wightman, was born in 1916. By then the family had moved to a handsome yellow frame house at No. 3 Charles Street. George had finished law school in 1914 and was practicing law when World War I intervened and he went into the service. During the war Hazel played "patriotic tennis," her description for the many fund-raising exhibition matches she played for the Red Cross.

In 1918, Hazel won the U.S. mixed doubles with Irving Wright. In 1919, sports rebounded from the grim war years in a hearty way. The transition paved the way for the Age of Sports. Hazel won her first national indoor titles, singles and doubles, in New York in February and later won the city's Metropolitan singles championship—after losing the first ten games in a row.

As Jack Dempsey prepared to fight Jess Willard for the heavyweight championship in Toledo, Hazel found time to play the nationals at the sedate Philadelphia Cricket Club again. This time she stunned everyone with a most convincing victory. Losing just one set on the way, she overwhelmed younger Marion Zinderstein, also of Boston, 6-1, 6-2 in the final. The *New York Times*, describing Hazel as "the stocky little player from the Hub" (failing to mention she was the mother of three), said she could have destroyed Molla Mallory, who had lost in the semis, and that her playing level had to rank alongside May Sutton Bundy and Mary Browne.

"Her tennis this week has been, if anything, superior to that which she displayed during her first term of supremacy," the *Times* said. "In fact, Mrs. Wightman admitted after the match that she felt today exactly as she did ten years ago when she first won the title."

The writer was impressed that Hazel hadn't "indulged" in interminable baseline dueling, depending on errors for points. Instead, like a chess master, she strategically moved in on short-ball opportunities to finish points at the net. Her workmanlike style was one that a tennis crowd in any era since would appreciate.

Hazel was through with singles after that. She was over thirty and three times a mother. Doubles, by comparison, was just half a court to cover and easier to manage. And it was the game she was truly meant to play. Hereafter, she would choose her tournaments and events carefully.

For old times' sake she paired with Wallace Johnson, her partner from 1909 and 1911, and for a third time they won the U.S. mixed doubles championships in 1920. That year was special. Because of an accidental meeting, it set her on a kind of mission as a talent scout for the rest of her life.

It had remained an annual tradition that Hazel and her family took the train back three thousand miles to Berkeley in late summer or early fall to visit for several weeks. It was an expensive journey in those days. In 1915, the family brought the strong young Molla Bjurstedt with them "to introduce her to the West," Hazel said. As a unique representative of both western and eastern tennis, Hazel already felt a maternal responsibility in the American tennis community. Identifying talent became one of her self-appointed tasks.

During her 1920 visit to Berkeley, Hazel walked a block over to the Berkeley Tennis Club. Among the kids practicing there she saw a young girl with pigtails. Her breath must have stopped, because this player impressed her as no youngster ever had before.

"I asked immediately to meet her," Hazel wrote in her book *Better Tennis*, "and we played several times together. Her physique and her concentration on the game were remarkable, and when I made suggestions, it was a delight to watch her immediate application of new ideas. A great desire to learn and an unswerving will to accomplish a definite job each day have been the chief reasons for her success. Always appreciative of her opponent, and unlike the average girl or boy of fourteen, who can seldom resist the temptation to waste time fooling on the tennis court, she played purposefully from the beginning. She never played too long at a time, however, so that she was always very keen. No one could have had more pleasure than I in watching her progress to the position of premiere woman tennis player of the world."

Her name was Helen Wills, and she was the daughter of a physician and his wife who lived nearby. Helen had been given a club membership for her thirteenth birthday and took up tennis as easily as she had art and even shooting lessons. But from the beginning she showed an extraordinary ability at the baseline to pound the ball without missing and to concentrate and shut everything out but the task at hand. Her behavior was completely unemotional and it took model behavior to the limits. Later, when she had gained international prominence that was to last into the late 1930s, she was known as "Little Miss Poker Face," a moniker the press had given the beautiful, icy queen of the sport. In the present professional arena, this motif would likely fuel a multimillion-dollar image in advertising.

Wills dominated tennis so thoroughly—eight Wimbledon singles titles and seven U.S. Championships—that her matches came to be viewed as executions. Wills's account of her initial meeting with Hazel Wightman appeared in a first-person story in the October 1977 *Reader's Digest*. Hazel's introducing herself was a turning point for both of them.

"At the mention of her name my eyes opened wide," Wills wrote. "Though only a fourteen-year-old novice, I was well aware that Mrs. Wightman was a four-time winner of the U.S. women's championship. But I couldn't begin to imagine how much this friendly little lady would show me, not only about backhand volleys but also about life and living. . . . The day after we met, my real tennis education began."

Hazel, thirty-three at the time, was visiting for six weeks, so there was a lot of time she could give to the eager, flawlessly polite child. Footwork rated a priority, because Wills wasn't a natural speedster as some of today's pros are. In fact, Hazel's impatient and repeated exhortations to "Run, Helen, run!" became part of Wills lore told by historians who compare champions down through the ages.

The most famous example was from the 1924 Paris Olympics, when Hazel and Helen were the winning team in doubles over the British. The story goes that Hazel repeatedly implored, "Run, Helen, run!" Wills later said she held back because she was a stickler about conserving energy on the court. She only ran when she absolutely had to. Even so, that didn't make her feet lighter. There is another famous story of a time when Helen and her mother stayed with the Wightmans, and Helen's noisy tromping down the stairs led Hazel to yell at her, "Helen! Please pick up those 9Bs!"

"If I made a silly mistake," Wills wrote of her mentor while remembering that summer of 1920, "she just looked away, her face assuming a patient but hopeful expression. But when I won a well-played point, she beamed so brightly that I wanted to please her every time."

Hazel taught Wills how to be patient with forehand exchanges and firm with the volley, as well as how to read the opposition. "I learned from her how to anticipate an opponent's shot by her position on the court and by the position of her body," Wills said. "She taught me to rivet my attention—'see only the ball'—and to stifle anger or elation as useless distractions."

For the observant teenager, Hazel herself became a study. Wills recalled a time the next summer, after winning the under-eighteen Pacific Coast title, when she and her mother went to Brookline to stay three weeks with Mrs. Wightman. Once, while driving to the courts, Hazel lost the diamond out of her engagement ring. Wills began searching the car frantically for it. "Not now," Hazel commanded. "First things first. We've got to practice." The two obviously shared a facility for single-mindedness.

Wills wasn't the only girl Hazel met when she came west. The older woman assumed a responsibility for meeting other promising girls who might earn trips east on their tennis results. Some had turned down expense-paid train trips to the East because they had no contacts on the distant shore to make them feel comfortable. Mrs. Wightman invited them to visit at No. 3

Charles Street and use her house as a base of operations. Her role as adviser expanded.

It was about this time that Hazel had a great idea. A name had risen in Europe, Suzanne Lenglen of France. Winning her first Wimbledon in 1919, Lenglen had never lost a match. As her record grew, so did curiosity about her on this side of the ocean. Lenglen believed tennis was meant to be graceful in the extreme. She had a fine tennis mind and used long and short diagonal shots to the best advantage. Close to the net she leapt for volleys and overheads like a ballerina, and in fact studied with the Russian Ballet in the South of France.

The French girl had written a sweet congratulatory note to Mrs. Wightman after Hazel's surprising win in the 1919 U.S. Championships. Now, too, several countries had strong women players. Why not, Hazel mused, have a national showdown like the men's Davis Cup? As her oldest daughter Virginia says, "She wanted for women what men had." By talking to the men about the Davis Cup, Hazel learned that they loved the experience, the travel, and meeting new players. The contest had improved the standard of men's tennis worldwide, and more than twenty countries were involved.

Chapter 5

THE WIGHTMAN CUP

The next week Hazel walked into N. G. Wood & Sons on Park Street in Boston. She had the image of the Davis Cup in mind, expecting to find some elegant silver urn or bowl to suitably proclaim the grandeur of a nation's worldwide dominance. She thought the U.S., Great Britain, France, and possibly Spain would field the pioneering teams. Maybe more countries would join if the idea really caught on.

All the shop had was a skinny, twenty-eight-inch high fluted cup more suitable for cut flowers than holding a victory champagne punch like the Davis Cup could. She plunked down three hundred dollars for it anyway. "By nature I'm a purchaser not a shopper," she later explained.

The bigger disappointment was that nothing happened. At the invitation, the countries fielding the Davis Cup teams demurred. They were either apathetic over the idea or thought putting money into a team would crimp their budgets for sending players abroad to compete internationally.

The cup that Hazel had the shop engrave simply "Challenge Cup—Ladies Team Match" sat and gathered dust. It was almost four years before Julian S. Myrick, a dynamic, ambitious man who ran an advertising agency with composer Charles Ives, dreamed up a proposal that eventually made the name Wightman one of the most recognized names on British and American newspaper sports pages.

The men's U.S. Championships were moved from the swank but less than commodious Newport Casino on Rhode Island to the grounds of the West Side Tennis Club in Forest Hills on Long Island in 1915. This was a major shift in how tennis was to be viewed outdoors. Additional changes would soon make America's premier tournament more accessible to ordinary people.

The Rhode Island seaside resort, long considered part of the Boston tennis scene, had had its problems. Tennis was considered an "in" thing for its wealthy vacationers. But when five thousand people went to the finals, the traffic and cacophony that their chugging, wheezing automobiles caused (before tops and windshields were standard equipment) were awful. There were no hotels either, so visitors paid exorbitant rents for rooms. Once inside the famous casino's gingerbread building, the crowds became irritatingly chatty. The scene was more social than sporting.

Julian Myrick had successfully lobbied the USLTA for the switch to the West Side Tennis Club, where he was a member and later president. It was quite a battle Myrick waged and a coup for New York, home of most of the nation's ranked top one hundred.

The liberating move to the West Side Tennis Club threw open the doors to the working stiff, providing he had the money for an admission ticket. In 1915, more than nine thousand attended the finals. Myrick was tournament chairman. The crowd was predominantly men. An aerial view of the audience showed a sea of boaters—those popular seasonal straw hats the men wore.

The women's championships were moved to Forest Hills in 1921. The gate-profitable men's championships rotated briefly then to Philadelphia before Myrick could wrest it back to the club in 1924. The men's finals could draw seven thousand at the West Side Tennis Club, but over a whole week in Philadelphia the event couldn't draw more than fourteen thousand. What did pack spectators in anywhere, however, was the Davis Cup, and that, too, is what the ambitious Myrick landed at Forest Hills the same year the women arrived, all apparently part of a trade-off.

After World War I, nationalism ran high. In 1920 Big Bill Tilden and Little Bill Johnston sailed to Australia, won the cup (which was actually contested in New Zealand), and brought it back amid great fanfare. The Davis Cup hit a popularity stride it would maintain for forty years. When the U.S. defended the cup against Japan in 1921 at the West Side Tennis Club, fourteen thousand spectators a day came through the gates. They sat crowded uncomfortably on bleachers erected on the club's adjacent courts. Clearly a stadium was needed. Women's matches didn't draw as well; 2,500 was about tops for a women's final. For the week of the 1921 championships, for example, attendance was 10,250.

Forest Hills, with its Tudor-style club, tidy houses, and red-roofed gables, could have been an old English hamlet. The setting was as quaint as Newport had been charming and elitist. But now tennis was more serious business than before. Money had wormed its way into this international game. Gates and profits were watchwords.

"The nature of the crowd seemed to be changing," Robert Minton wrote in *Forest Hills: An Illustrated History*. "Instead of reporting the names of boxholders who were socially prominent, the West Side Club sent out a list of [tennis] notables attending the Davis Cup matches . . . players, organizers, and supporters of the game. The Newport image was fading as the game became a national undertaking of real importance."

It hadn't gone unnoticed in America that Wimbledon had put up a stadium in 1922 in anticipation of the crowds that would come to see France's invincible Suzanne Lenglen play. But what decided the issue of whether to build a stadium at Forest Hills in 1923 was the continued success of the men's Davis Cup. Tilden and company ended up winning the cup a record seven straight years, 1920–1926.

Myrick had always liked Hazel's mothballed idea and was looking for a christening act for the new stadium. He decided on the first women's international challenge cup for that purpose. Hazel had never proposed the idea as "the Wightman Cup," yet that's what it was called in the *New York Times* from the very first weekend, a tidy title with a touch of human interest. The more impersonal "Challenge Cup—Ladies Team Match" is what Hazel had engraved on the fluted trophy, with the Wightman name nowhere on it. Ironically, it had been the same when Dwight Filley Davis, a twenty-one-year-old recent Harvard graduate and a top player, bought a sterling silver bowl and called it the International Lawn Tennis Challenge Trophy. Beginning play in 1900, he intended for the yearly event, which involved the teams of several countries, to advance international goodwill. But for the first three years only Great Britain competed with the U.S., and the bowl came quickly to be known as the Davis Cup.

Hazel sought no publicity for herself; she just wanted the leading ladies from around the globe to get to know one another and enjoy a success like the Davis Cup, which had grown quite successful and then boasted a field of twenty countries. "The first Wightman Cup match was hastily cooked up," *The New Yorker*'s Herbert Warren Wind wrote in *The Fireside Book of Tennis*. "Work on the new stadium at the West Side Tennis Club in Forest Hills had been completed that summer, and the USLTA was pondering a distinguished opening event when someone remembered that a group of England's best women players was on its way across the Atlantic to play in our tournaments, and someone else remembered the Wightman Cup. In a ship-to-shore exchange of radiograms, an international match, England versus the United States, was arranged for Forest Hills to begin on August 10."

Another account by Robert Minton in *Forest Hills: An Illustrated History*, explains the invitation this way: "On his own initiative, Myrick proceeded to wire Mrs. Wightman that the club was prepared to launch her international series of team matches in the new stadium." The contest would begin with Great Britain, "the challenger," and later expand to other countries. What in fact occurred was rather the opposite of what Hazel had in mind.

"When I gave the cup," Hazel said to $American Heritage, "I thought it would be nice to see that French girl, Suzanne Lenglen, come over here. She won Wimbledon in 1919, and I won the National here in 1919. Everybody thought it was quite something to win the Nationals in 1909 and ten years later to win it again. But I never thought of any such thing. I just thought wouldn't it be fun to have Suzanne Lenglen and other foreigners come here to play. But the English women had no desire to compete in anything with the French at the time."

The Brits' anti-French and anti-outsider stance persisted over the years when others wanted in. Hazel described the attitude in her diplomatic way as "Interesting. Small. But there was nothing you could do about it. I didn't worry about it."

For the competition format itself, Hazel had conceived of something slightly different from the Davis Cup. She used the best of seven matches, maybe because the World Series was seven games, or because it would just involve more people and be merrier. It was five singles and two doubles, as opposed to the Davis Cup's four singles and one doubles. She selected Molla

Mallory, Helen Wills, Eleanor Goss, and herself as the team.

Oddly, Hazel chose Wills to play number two ahead of Goss, despite the young girl's inexperience and loss to Goss just a few days earlier. It was no oversight. Hazel was pushing on the girl, and it paid off.

"I was surprised, for I had thought that if I were to be on the team at all, I would be third," Wills wrote in her autobiography. "Looking back, I can see that, mingled with my feelings of surprise and pleasure at being placed in the No. 2 position on the team, there was a new feeling of confidence in my game. I felt that I had been admitted to the ranks of the leading players."

On August 11, construction that had started in April wasn't quite finished on the fourteen-thousand-seat horseshoe bowl. About five thousand came anyway, and there was plenty of room. The stadium was 195 feet long and 145 feet wide, forming a U around three grass courts. Like the Roman Coliseum, rows of seats began above a ten-feet-high wall. At the open end to the east was an awning-covered marquee area for officials, press, and players. For more than half a century Forest Hills would be America's tennis capital.

That first year the Wightman Cup, held the weekend of August 11-12, 1923, competed with the popular Ziegfeld Follies, the Yankee's home-run-hitting Babe Ruth, Gloria Swanson in "Blue Beard's Eighth Wife," Jeanne Eagles in "Rain," and, on Saturday, a national day of mourning for President Warren Harding.

On opening day, four trumpeters began the ceremony on top of the promenade, playing the national anthems of both countries, whose flags flew majestically. The players entered reverently. USLTA vice president George Wightman, ready to take over from president and Davis Cup founder Dwight Davis the next year, gave a speech of welcome. The American and British captains sat on either side of the umpire's stand. Coaching was permitted. Hazel advised Wills to "use your head and be patient." "For a young person about to play in her first international match," Wills said years later, "this simple bit of advice was the best that could have been offered."

Hailed as the likely successor to Suzanne Lenglen, seventeen-year-old Helen Wills defeated Kitty McKane 6-2, 7-5 after coming back in the second set from 2-5, 15-40, double-set point. Hazel—the playing captain—and Eleanor Goss then squeaked by Miss McKane and Phyllis Covell 10-8, 5-7, 6-4 to win a doubles point. Hazel gave "a thrilling display" of her doubles expertise in "sharp rallies and dashing play," according to the *New York Times*. The U.S. shut out the British 7-0 as the U.S. women's championship singles matches began simultaneously on the outside courts.

From that weekend forth, one writer from the *London Daily Telegram* wrote, "the name of Hazel Wightman became the driving inspiration for generation after generation of British school girls who hoped for ultimate success at tennis." Wills observed that after that first doubles match, "she [Mrs. Wightman] earned such a reputation for doubles generalship that the English teams we met in following years were defeated almost before they went on the court."

As a result of her Wightman Cup experience, Wills was never the same player. "It was my first big win in the senior field and, at the same time, marked the day when I entered the realm of international tennis," she wrote. "It was a turning point in my game." People attributed the teenager's discipline on and off the court to a strict mother. But it was actually Wills who imposed demands on herself and insisted her mother help enforce them to such an extent it quite amused Hazel Wightman. Hazel would often ask Mrs. Wills in jest if she was still "in training."

A week later, ever heeding Hazel's advice to "use your head and be patient," Wills upset Molla Mallory to become champion of the United States. Over several years she went on to become one of the greatest women players of all time and in one four-and-a-half year stretch of no losses at all was completely invincible as "Queen Helen." Exciting as the Wightman Cup week may have been in Hazel's life, it was actually the next year, 1924, fifteen years after her first national singles title, that became the pinnacle of her playing career. It was the Olympics in Paris. She was one of the oldest athletes there. And she won two gold medals.

Chapter 6

LIFE WITH GEORGE, THE 1924 OLYMPICS

It was quite a life, a storybook existence, and Hazel had worked hard for her many and distinguished accomplishments. In her modest and simple way, she had used determination and analysis to get the most out of her game. And she gave one hundred percent in life away from the court, too, using the same disarming style. She couldn't be labeled because there was no type, no mold, for the role she played in American tennis. She was the frontier woman.

Hazel evolved in a rare time. Before she began to have an influence on the game, tennis was about as elitist as it ever has been. But at the same time a limited number of public parks were making a tremendous contribution. The finest example was Golden Gate Park. Its courts were the home of champions Maurice McLoughlin and Little Bill Johnston and several others who followed them at the inviting public facility that eastern writers said had "democratized" the sport. People's origins made no difference to Hazel. Tennis was tennis, and it was good. And it was an option for everyone.

George Wightman was a very successful attorney, and the income was substantial. Household help was employed. Regardless, Hazel strove to be the perfect housekeeper herself, and without shame or embarrassment she was true to many habits from early farm influences. She offered snacks of her baked brownies as well as dried prunes and raisins, to the hordes that came to visit.

George was an expert at court tennis, that anachronistic forebear of lawn tennis that had been developed, it is believed, by the French. Played indoors under a high ceiling, court tennis players used funny bent rackets to knock a hard ball over a long, saggy net. The net, very high on the sides and quite low in the middle, draped eerily down from the walls, where it was attached like a mutant spider's web.

George competed regularly at an exclusive downtown Boston men's club, the Tennis and Racquet Club, which celebrated his titles and adroitness with a wall plaque. Naturally, Hazel wanted to try this old court version. Anything that had to do with rackets and paddles intrigued her. But like many men of the time, George held absolute ideas about honor and dignity on and off the playing fields, and about precious male domains. Court tennis was his. So Hazel was denied. It remained his separate activity.

Even after they had moved to Charles Street, the Wightman family mansion continued to be part of their lives. All the adults in the family, for example, gathered there for Wednesday dinner. Adults and children assembled there for Sunday dinner, when there was a lot of family activity. The children loved the place. The marble floor of the foyer was perfect for a great run and slide, not to mention the ecstasies of the massive, curling oak banisters. For winter vacations, everyone went to Palm Beach, Florida. On the Hotchkiss side, every other summer, Hazel and her children vacationed for several weeks with her family in Berkeley. George usually had to leave after a week or so to return to work.

Meanwhile, Hazel Wightman's reputation in tennis grew. It now bridged a second generation and, with the Wightman Cup, spread across a second continent. The second year of cup competition, 1924, was played at Wimbledon the week before the All-England Championships. The United States did not fare well at all. Young Helen Wills lost both of her singles matches. Everyone else lost, too, except for the lone doubles match that Hazel, the team's playing captain, salvaged with Helen Wills. Hazel was thirty-seven, Wills seventeen, both having after-the-season birthdays. After leading Kitty McKane 6-4, 4-1, Wills lost the next week in the Wimbledon singles final and wept. It was the only time she ever lost at Wimbledon, and it was the last time, too, she ever cried over a match. She decided thereafter to add a stiff upper lip to her already remarkably cool behavior, which, as she became invincible over the years, continued to attract almost as much petty criticism as praise. Perhaps as a result of her famous poise, her concentration became at least the equal of Hazel's.

Helen and Hazel went on to win the Wimbledon doubles over a tough British tandem, Kitty McKane and Phyllis Covell. The five-foot-eight inch Wills laced pinpoint returns from the backcourt, and diminutive, nimble Hazel darted about the net to put away volleys, occasionally directing her heavy-footed partner as to positioning. They were a superb team of power, accuracy, and daring and were never defeated.

Playing in the singles draw without much hope for the title, Hazel ran up against Suzanne Lenglen and was trounced 6-0, 6-0. The French girl, who didn't hesitate to say nice things about Hazel's game, then fell ill and had to default, ending her quest for a sixth straight title in a run that had begun in 1919. That had been the year Hazel became the inspiration of women athletes in America, showing them they could pause for motherhood and then return to their beloved sport successfully. Hazel, thirty-two and the mother of three children, had won the 1919 U.S. Championships, inspiring the young Lenglen to write her a congratulatory note from an ocean away.

In Paris in the summer of 1924, one of the most memorable Olympic Games in modern history was held. It has inspired memoirs and movies ever since, and Hazel Wightman and Helen Wills both covered themselves in glory there. Wills salvaged her Wimbledon singles loss by winning the Olympic gold medal in singles, Hazel won two gold medals, and, together again, Helen and Hazel won the doubles over the British.

The U.S. team, men and women, made a complete sweep of Olympic tennis in 1924. What proved to be the most interesting part was the mixed doubles. Hazel played with R. Norris "Dick" Williams, a Philadelphia player who had been educated in Europe and at Harvard. Fluent in French and voted by the players the most popular, Williams was an erratic hit or miss power player who, when on, was practically unbeatable. He had twice won the NCAA singles and doubles. Even more remarkable was that while he was still at Harvard in 1914, he had won the U.S. Championships by upsetting the world's number one Maurice McLoughlin. This was two years after Williams had survived the sinking of the *Titanic*, which claimed his father's life.

Among the athletes on the U.S. Olympic team were sprinter Charlie

Paddock, revered as the fastest human alive, and Johnny Weissmuller, who would prove the fastest swimmer and later became a movie legend as the inscrutable, stentorian Tarzan of the Apes. Also competing was an eleven-year-old dimpled doll from Oslo named Sonja Henie, who went on to ice-skate her way professionally to a $47.5 million fortune.

Hazel was not the oldest gold medal winner that year, either. A forty-year-old sewing machine salesman, Albin Steenroos from Helsinki, won the marathon in this, the dramatic Olympics that inspired the making of the popular Hollywood movie *Chariots of Fire* sixty years later.

George Wightman was USLTA president then. Additionally, he served on the 1924 U.S. Olympic committee along with General Douglas MacArthur. It may have appeared self-serving to some that George's wife was selected for the Olympic team, but it wasn't at all. Hazel, who, unlike most women then, cleanly put away just about all her overhead smashes, was still likely the nation's leading doubles player and as such, according to Wills, she infused a magical confidence in all her partners. Besides, it was economical to send the Wightman Cup team at Wimbledon on to Colombes, France.

On the outskirts of Paris, Colombes was a dusty manufacturing district dotted with dirty cafes and grimy buildings. What greeted the team when they first arrived and viewed the court site was a Fellini-like surrealism. In the background, where roaring crescendos of approval would soon erupt, was a large stadium in a barren field overgrown with dry weeds and stickers. Close to it, anxious for their moment in the spotlight, brawny wrestlers practiced on a platform, and on a frame of rods and bars, chiseled gymnasts polished their daring feats of precision. In the foreground was the shocking sight of pyramid piles of red clay and sand—the tennis courts.

"The courts were laid in time, however," Helen Wills said. "It seems to be the French way to work to the last minute, and even a little after, if necessary. The stands were completed, too, finally. The dressing room for the women players was a large shed with a tin roof and had in it a shower that worked in only one needle. There was much complaint at the poor arrangements." Once laid, the courts dried out quickly due to hot weather. They became very fast and irritatingly dusty, almost unplayable when they were windswept.

Not in attendance were the world's two best players, the ailing Suzanne Lenglen (jaundice) and Bill Tilden. The U.S. had two teams in the mixed doubles finals. The question was whether the match needed to be played, since Dick Williams was severely injured. Tilden, who had always said Williams's biggest drawback as a player was lazy feet, should have seen the match that finally did transpire, for it was Williams at his slowest.

Williams held some quixotic notions about tennis style. He wouldn't scramble awkwardly for a ball at the expense of his sweeping, nice-looking form. He had lost matches because of it. Among his peers, he alone thought the typical no-man's-land mid-court area was a good spot from which to volley. And in mixed doubles, his chivalry was unparalleled. He didn't think it ethical to lob a woman opponent who was facing the sun.

These attitudes apparently did not hinder Hazel's ability to adjust. She had her hands full with a more serious matter: Williams, who usually played two feet inside the baseline and hit hard and flat, couldn't move at all because he had a broken Achilles tendon, suffered in the previous round.

He and Hazel faced men's singles winner Vinnie Richards and his partner Marion Jessup. It's amazing Williams even took the court, allowing Hazel to assume such a great burden. But she, as an older woman, must have convinced him that a default would have deprived her of the kind of ultimate challenge she relished most. Williams had to stand in one spot, at the net or in the backcourt, hitting only balls he could reach in one step. He couldn't push off. Of course at the net he was a sitting duck for lobs. Never mind. Hazel, anticipating them, would pick up her skirts and dash back to cover anything over his head. They won rather handily, too, 6-2, 6-3. Even the small, pencil-thin ballboys, who usually spent their spare time beneath the bleachers eating lemons, came out to watch the sight. And a peregrinating knot of UC Berkeley students and athletes showed up to add the school's favorite "Oski-wow-wow" cheer of encouragement, which must have mystified the rude audience that booed about every close call.

"All Dick could do was return the serve and then hobble to the net," Hazel said in a 1972 taped interview, "and I would take his lobs and the short chops hit to him. I don't know how I did it, but I did."

Years later, Williams confessed he was not only gimpy but grumpy then, too. The tournament, from its trappings to its officiating, galled him. In a commemorating speech pointing out Hazel's extraordinary powers of concentration, he recalled:

"We played our matches in the Olympics under the worst conditions imaginable. The French completed the courts barely three days before the tournament began, so a fine spray of dust blew in our faces all week. The main stadium, where the track and field events were going on, directly adjoined the tennis courts, and there was no knowing when a pistol would suddenly go off, or a national anthem blare forth, or just some announcement bellowed or rebellowed in several languages.

"The officials running the tennis tournament allowed vendors to circulate all over the stadium and to hawk their oranges, bananas, and ice cream at the top of their lungs. On top of this, the officiating was really the poorest I have ever encountered. On several days only the umpire showed up and the line judges had to be recruited from patrons in the stands. I was on edge the entire tournament, but nothing bothered Hazel, nothing at all. I don't think she even heard them selling those bananas."

Perhaps these little-known hardships, the awareness of her age, the worldly platform and press ballyhoo surrounding the games, and the emotion of national anthems played for triumphant athletes—the memory of all that—made her answer "the Olympics" when in later years she was repeatedly asked what her greatest career thrill had been.

Tennis was gone from the Olympics after 1924. The bad conditions in France contributed to the decision, of course. But the warring between amateur tennis associations and the Olympic committee couldn't be quelled. The committee wanted the Olympics known as "the championship of the world." The associations said no. If any event deserved that title it was Wimbledon in the British Empire, where the lawn sport was born. The associations wouldn't hear otherwise.

Tennis stayed out of the Olympics for the next sixty-four years. That made Hazel and Helen Wills and the rest of the winning Americans the longest titleholders in Olympic history. More impressive, and lost in obscurity, was the fact Hazel had won two gold medals as a thirty-seven-year-old mother of four.

In 1990, however, Hazel became the first tennis player ever featured on a U.S. Post Office stamp. It was on a commemorative series honoring posthumously five extraordinary Olympic stars from the first half of the century. The other four were sprinter Jesse Owens, boxer and bobsledder Eddie Eagan, swimmer Helene Madison, and high jumper Ray Ewry.

Nationwide, the stamp announcement popped up as little stories and "mentions" in the print media. But in Healdsburg, Hazel's childhood home and the community that had placed a plaque in its plaza honoring Hazel in 1963, it was front-page headlines in the *Herald*. From the Northern California Tennis Hall of Fame to the halls of the University of California, from the Los Angeles Tennis Club to the Berkeley Tennis Club, the West, which has less of a claim on her, still holds on to her dearly.

Although the Olympics capped Hazel's year, it didn't end it. To be sure, 1924 was one of those seasons with numerous, unexpected peaks of marvelous tennis experiences. One was royal. For some reason, this was one of the few of Hazel's anecdotes in which she liked name-dropping. Perhaps it was because the episode had a family theme to it and because people could read into it small, implied lessons about life.

Stopping on the way home from the Olympics in San Sebastian, Spain, she and a few of the team were invited by the American ambassador, Alexander Moore, to come to the Spanish king's summer palace and play some tennis with the royal family, which they did. Hazel gave a brief account of the episode in *American Heritage* magazine (August 1975) and obviously enjoyed it.

On court in the royal gardens, the king had asked if she would play doubles by teaming with his second son, Don Jaime. "I think you can take my second son and win a match from my number-one son [the prince of Asturias] and his cousin," the king said to her. "You're the only person I've ever seen that might be able to do this favor for me. Will you play?"

Although Hazel was unsure what etiquette was expected in this unfolding scene, hell had a better chance of freezing over than of her declining this once-in-a-lifetime challenge. Despite her tall partner's youthful and awkward aggressiveness—and inability to hear the authoritative albeit non-royal command of "Mine!"—they did prevail, although Hazel got bonked on the head a couple of times. She was relieved when it was over.

The king was delighted. In the next set Hazel played mixed doubles with Julian S. Myrick, the men's Olympic captain, against Queen Victoria Eugenia and Vinnie Richards. Earlier, when they were descending the palace steps, the queen had said she wasn't going to play because she didn't think she was good enough. "But when I protested," Hazel later wrote, "she called to one of her children as simply as any mother would, 'Beatrice, go back and get my tennis shoes.'

"The Queen Mother was impressed when she heard that I had four children—my daughter Dorothy was a baby then. To both of us, our families were more important than anything else in the world, and we had a good time talking about them."

Finding themselves up 5-3, Hazel suggested quietly to Myrick that out of politeness they ought to find a discreet way to narrowly lose to the queen, which they did. "When we got through playing," Hazel recalled, "I sat down next to the king—oh, he was a cute old fellow—and he said, 'Well, I've never seen a match thrown so beautifully.'"

It was about the only time in her life that she gracefully backed off from her competitive fire. All of her life, her nature drove her to thump her grandchildren in parlor games, to dominate at bridge tables, even to take the Massachusetts state table tennis title and, once each, the national squash and badminton titles in the late 1920s—just to show she could do it. Anything with a racket attracted her, she used to say. "I was never a golf player. I played once, and I got a top score. It just happened. But I don't like any game that's slow."

Back home, at the U.S. Championships in 1924, she and Helen Wills ended their perfect year with the ladies' doubles crown. Women's tennis was continuing to grow then. More and more, credit for it was given unequivocally to Hazel and her unceasing influence. At the Berkeley Tennis Club in the summer of 1923, for example, Hazel had met and encouraged the young, talented Berkeley teenager Helen Jacobs. They worked together three mornings a week. Jacobs, too, listened as if Hazel's words had risen off a stone tablet and rumbled down from a mountaintop, an attitude that led Hazel to declare rather lavishly, given her egalitarianism: "Helen Jacobs was the most responsive, and in a way, the most satisfying pupil I've ever taught."

But Hazel couldn't get the two Helens to practice together. The girls feuded in a chilly, barely discernible, yet irreparable personality clash that followed them all their lives. Hazel gave up after two tries. Of course Jacobs was just fourteen then, and Wills, the national junior champion and women's runner-up, was on her way to becoming the nation's women's champion that year at seventeen. Hazel saw no conflict or danger in generously dispensing her care and coaching to both.

In August of 1924, the California Tennis Association chose Jacobs to represent the state at the national junior tournament in Philadelphia. Routed through Canada, it took the anxious teenager and her mother nine days by train to travel the three thousand miles to Boston, their first eastern destination, where she would play a warm-up tournament. There, Hazel waited for them on the platform.

"Hers was a welcome and exciting presence," Jacobs later wrote of the time in her biography, "for she became at once the link between me and my adventures. It was she who had advised the tennis association to send my entry to the Longwood tournament, and it was she who later took me to New York to see the Johnston-Tilden final in the 1924 National Championships—the greatest display of tennis I have ever seen. It was she, too, who took Mother and me under her wing when we were fatigued from our trip and installed us as her guests in her house in Brookline.

"Number 3 Charles Street was the scene of my introduction to the first international champions I had ever met, with the exception of the Californians, Bill Johnston and Helen Wills." There, wide-eyed and courteous, Jacobs met Tilden and the amusing and chatty Jean Borotra, a volatile and charming French star who punctuated his spirited conversations with delicious French phrases.

Jacobs won her first national juniors then. Bill Tilden declared in his 1925 book that Hazel, besides being "the greatest of all women net players," was the major influence in developing women players in America. He went on to say, "California has led the way in women's tennis in the United States. Every year sees new and interesting young players come east." Four years before, Wills had come east as a youngster with pigtails, and, Tilden wrote, "today she is conceded to be one of the greatest players of all time." Jacobs, whom he called a "husky little miss of sixteen" was a fiery type who reminded him of McLoughlin, and he predicted she'd go far. New York, Philadelphia, and Boston, he said, had produced few players until the last five years. He said it was due to the successes of Molla Mallory and "the return to competition and wonderful personal interest of Mrs. Hazel Wightman," plus the work she and Florence Ballin did organizing and developing women's tournaments.

I. Hazel: early days and family

Hazel 1907.

Hazel 1909
at Coronado, CA.

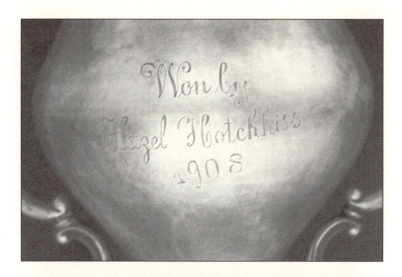

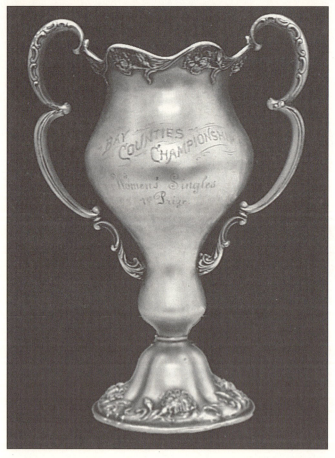

Hazel, Ethel Sutton, May Sutton, and Florence Sutton.

About 1900
Lucretia Hite Grove,
Hazel's grandmother.

James Rankin Grove,
Hazel's grandfather.

About 1925
Emma Grove Hotchkiss,
Hazel's mother.

W. J. Hotchkiss,
Hazel's father.

3 Generations of the Hotchkiss Family at their Ranch Home near Healdsburg, CA; about 1890, Left to right:
Front Row: Hazel, Linville; Middle row: James Miller, Marius, Homer
Back row: W. J. (William Josephus), Emma; To the side: Virginia, Benoni, unknown.

About 1863
Virginia, W. J. and Janie
(Hazel's grandmother,
father and aunt).

Berkeley home from about 1902 to death of both W. J. and Emma in 1936.

Hazel and brothers about 1905. Back row: Miller, Homer, Marius
Front row: Linville, Hazel.

Emma Grove Hotchkiss at 1924 Democratic convention.

II. Hazel 1910–1924

About 1910
Hazel and Maurice McLoughlin.

U. S. National Championship (1911)
Hazel in far court and Florence Sutton in near court.

1912 Hazel and George Wightman at Berkeley house, at time of wedding.

1914 Hazel and daughter Virginia.

1916 Hazel and children.

About 1918 Hazel and children.

(Left) Molla Bjurstedt Mallory (Right) Suzanne Lenglen.

1924 Wimbledon: Hazel and Helen Wills on the far side. They won the doubles that year.

Inscribed on back: "With pleasant recollections of our voyage home"
signed by Julian S. Myrick "On board Aquitania 1924"
Julian S. Myrick is third from left in back row
In front of him are Hazel and Helen.

At Wimbledon 5 July 1924. *Back row:* Julian S. Myrick; *Front row:* Vinnie Richards, Frank Hunter, Dick Williams, and Waddie Washburn.

The Spanish royal family at lunch after the 1924 Olympics.

III. The Family

About 1926 at W. J. Hotchkiss House
2985 Claremont Avenue, Berkeley, California.

Standing left to right:

Miller F. Hotchkiss (Marius' son)
Linville Hotchkiss (Hazel's brother)
Helena (Crusius) Hotchkiss
    (Marius' wife)
Margaret (Locan) Hotchkiss
    (Linville's wife)
Margaretta (Wilson) Hotchkiss
    (J. Miller's wife)
Hazel (Hotchkiss) Wightman
J. Miller Hotchkiss (Hazel's brother)
George Wightman, Hazel's son
George William Wightman,
    Hazel's husband
Marius Hotchkiss (Hazel's brother)

Middle Row:

Bill Hotchkiss (J. Miller's son)
Emma (Grove) Hotchkiss
    (Hazel's mother)
    holding Bill Wightman (Hazel's son)
W. J. (Joe) Hotchkiss (Hazel's father)
John Peter Hotchkiss (Linville's son)

Front Row:

Hazel Wightman (Hazel's daughter)
Dorothy Wightman
    (Hazel's daughter)
Virginia Wightman
    (Hazel's daughter)

They called themselves the ten grandchildren of W. J. Hotchkiss. Included are Hazel's five children: George, Hazel, Virginia, Dotty and Bill.

Miller, George, Emmy Lou, Hazel, Virginia, Bill, Pete, Dotty, Bill, Jim.

About 1931
Wightman family group with Helen Wills
Back row: Helen Wills, Virginia, George, Hazel (daughter)
Front row: Bill, Hazel (mother), Dorothy.

The New Year's calendar was a Wightman family tradition for many years. Following are three examples:

Year 1931 (the five children) Bill, Dorothy, Hazel, Virginia, George.

Year 1932 (five children and both parents)
Back row: George, Virginia, Hazel (mother), Hazel, George (father),
Front row: Bill, Dorothy.

Year 1935 (same group as 1932)
Back row: Virginia, George (father), George, Hazel
Front row: Dorothy, Hazel (mother), Bill.

IV. Later Life

The following three pictures were taken December, 1963 at the monument in Healdsburg, CA, which at that time had a living flame. It honored Healdsburg's four Olympic champions.

Hazel seated with her plaque visible.

Hazel standing.

Margaret (Grove) Luce, Hazel, Mary Jane (Miller) Grove, who was born 25 Nov 1864, Eva Lee (Grove) Calhoun. Margaret and Eva Lee are daughters of Mary Jane and Luther Grove. Luther was the brother of Emma (Grove) Hotchkiss. Thus, Mary Jane was Hazel's aunt. Margaret and Eva Lee were Hazel's first cousins.

About 1967 Hazel on steps at Longwood, at her favorite activity, making out a tournament list.

Hazel portrait maybe 1970 or earlier.
Note tennis bracelets. (*See next photo*).Currently on display at the
International Tennis Hall of Fame, Newport, Rhode Island.
Also note medal-Honorary Commander of the
Order of the British Empire. Currently on display at the Women's Collegiate
Tennis Hall of Fame, Williamsburg, Virginia.

Dorothy (Wightman) Hood speaking at inauguration ceremony May 24, 1978 University of California Women Athletes Hall of Fame.
(Note tennis bracelet).

Special exhibit Summer 1999 at Healdsburg Historical Society.

Special exhibit Summer 1999 at Healdsburg Historical Society.

Inauguration Ceremony
University of California Berkeley

Alumni House   **May 24, 1978**

Program for University of California inauguration ceremony May 24, 1978. The Hazel Hotchkiss Wightman Tennis Scholarship Fund was established at this time. It was the first women's tennis scholarship at the University.

Hazel and Chris Evert probably 1973 at Longwood.
(Notice tennis bracelets and O.B.E. medal.)

1974 signed first day cover Wightman Tennis Center.

Hazel and daughter Dorothy admiring a few of Hazel's tennis trophies.

Post card of Hazel Hotchkiss Wightman Tennis Center.

Hazel, Sally and Baysie 1974 newspaper photo. Baysie and Hazel may be
the only grandmother and granddaughter team in the world
to each have a New Yorker feature article.
(For Baysie's article see page 78, March 17, 1997.)

MRS. WIGHTMAN with sons in 1952, after winning her 43rd national title, the Women's Senior Doubles.

EMBASSY OF THE
UNITED STATES OF AMERICA

London, June 13th, 1938

Dear Mrs. Wightman:

    I want to extend to you and to the members of your team our heartiest congratulation on the magnificent playing last week. We all like our side to win, of course, but sometimes the manner of winning is even more gratifying than victory itself. From what I saw of the matches on Friday and from what I have heard from other spectators I gathered that our girls played beautifully and in a most sportsmanlike manner. Their visit here has been a source of pride to all Americans.

    With best wishes, I am,

                      Very sincerely yours,

                        Joseph P. Kennedy

Mrs. George W. Wightman,
    Hyde Park Hotel,
        Knightsbridge,
           S. W. 1.

Letter from American Ambassador Joseph P. Kennedy.

V. Wightman Cup

Performers in the first Wightman Cup Matches held in the inaugural event at the newly elected West Side Tennis Stadium at Forest Hills in 1923. Far court, British players Mrs. W. Geraldine Beamish and Mrs. R. C. Clayton were defeated by the U. S. Tandem, Mrs. Molla B. Mallory and Helen Wills. Circled, left column, top to bottom; Mrs. Molla B Mallory, Eleanor Goss, and Helen Wills. On the right, top to bottom, Kathleen McKane, Mrs. W. Geraldine Beamish, Mrs. R. C. Clayton. Donor and first U. S. Captain Mrs. George W. Wightman with trophy. U. S. won 7-0.

1929 U. S. and BRITISH TEAMS. Front row, U. S. team: Edith Cross, Helen Wills, Helen Jacobs, Mrs. H. H. Wightman. Back row, Mrs. B. C. Covell, Mrs. Peggy Saunders Michell, Betty Nuthall, Mrs. D. C. Shepherd-Barron, Mrs. Phoebe Watson.

1933 WIGHTMAN CUP TEAMS. Left to right, standing: Dorothy E. Round, Mrs. Peggy Saunders Mitchell, Margaret Scriven, non-playing Captain Malcolm Hern, Mrs. Helen Wills Moody, Holcombe Ward, Mrs. Hazel Wightman, Mrs. Marjorie Gladman Van Ryn, Alice Marble. Seated, from left: Betty Nuthall, Freda James, Mary Heeley, Sarah Palfrey, and Carolin Babcock.

LAST U. S. WIGHTMAN (1939) TEAM until after the war in '46. Left to right: Helen Jacobs, Alice Marble, Mrs. Hazel Wightman, Mary Arnold, Mrs. Sarah Palfrey Fayban, and Dorothy M. Bundy.

AGAIN IN '50. U. S. won every match at Wimbledon. Hart, Todd, Brough and duPont with Mrs. Wightman.

1953 U. S. TEAM. Left to right: Doris Hart, Shirley Fry, Captain Mrs. Margaret Osborne duPont, Maureen Connolly, and Louise Brough.

1965 U. S. SQUAD. From left: Susman, Varner, Captain duPont, Mrs. Wightman, Mrs. Carole Caldwell Graebner, Mrs. Billie Jean Moffitt King. Seated: Richey and Julie Heldman.

VI. From Hazel's book and Longwood program for the Fiftieth Anniversary of the Wightman Cup

To Hazel Hotchkiss Wightman:

"With much love to the best doubles player in the world, on this happy day at the Longwood Cricket Club. Do you remember we won every doubles match we ever played — because of you!

Wish I could be there today. My thoughts are with you — and my affection always."

Helen Wills Roark

At Del Monte CA, about 1908
Maurice McLaughlin is fourth in the front row,
Florence Sutton sixth, and Hazel seventh.

Sarah Palfrey.

Helen Wills.

"The Backhand" illustration from Hazel's book, *Better Tennis*.

1924 Doubles Champions
Hazel (r) and Helen Wills (l).

Hazel serving.

VII. Miscellany

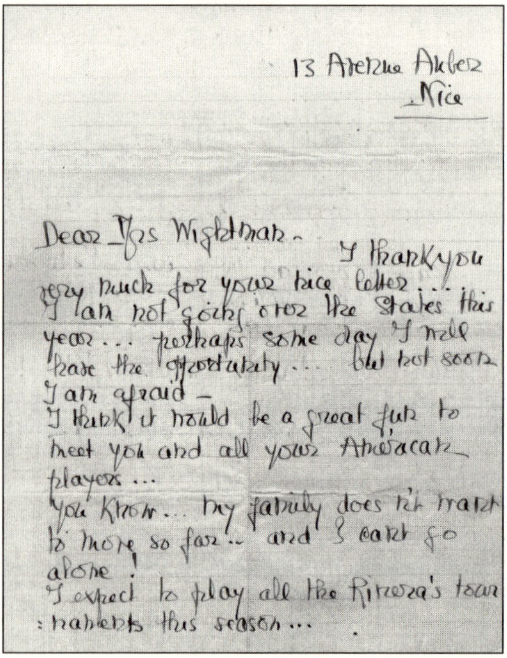

13 Avenue Auber
Nice

Dear Mrs Wightman -
I thank you very much for your nice letter...
I am not going over the States this year... perhaps some day I will have the opportunity... but not soon I am afraid -
I think it would be a great fun to meet you and all your American players...
You know... my family does not want to move so far... and I can't go alone!
I expect to play all the Riviera's tournaments this season...

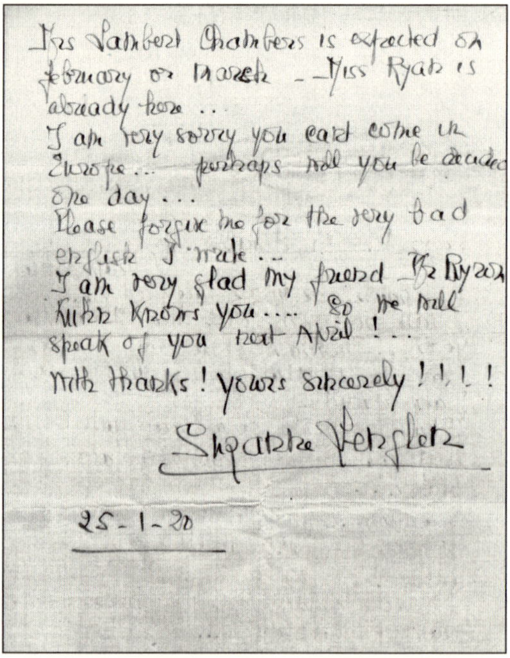

Mrs Lambert Chambers is expected on february or march - Miss Ryan is already here..
I am very sorry you can't come in Europe... perhaps will you be decided one day...
Please forgive me for the very bad english I write..
I am very glad my friend Mr Myers [illegible] knows you.... So we will speak of you next April!..
With thanks! yours sincerely!!!!

Suzanne Lenglen

25-1-20

Letter from Suzanne Lenglen.

THE TENNIS SONG
by MARY J. LYNCH

Dedicated to Mrs. Hazel Wightman

free Gift offer <u>on back</u>

nordyke

50¢ SONGS MUSI

Hazel and Arthur Ashe.

12 February '68

Dear Mrs. Weightman,

So good to hear from you. It's not often people of your stature stop and drop me a line. I do appreciate it. As for my turning professional, rest assured I won't tell I feel I'm ready. With Army duty and no major title under my belt I have a lot more "amateur" time left in me.

I feel the game is undergoing a change for the better. The public, I mean the working man, will now get exposed to this great game. This does not detract from the game as it is, it only adds to it. If you could believe the 23,000 people to see tennis in February in Philadelphia last weekend, you wouldn't believe your eyes. That's what we need — 23,000 people saw tennis over 3 days at the Spectrum Arena.

Thanks for your interest. See you at the Doubles.

Yours,
Arthur

100

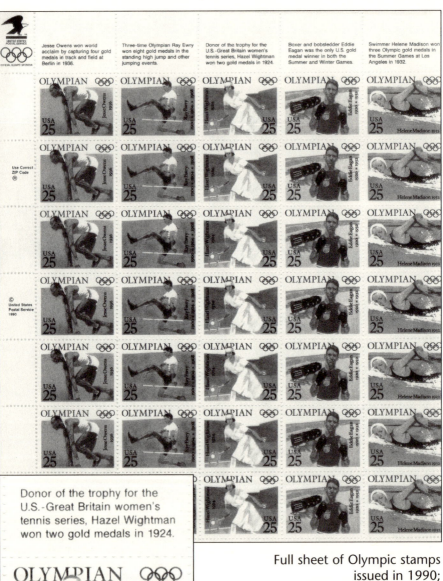

Full sheet of Olympic stamps
issued in 1990;
also a close-up of Hazel.
She is the only tennis player
ever honored on a US stamp.

Chapter 7

SARAH PALFREY

"ONE CANNOT OVERESTIMATE THE SERVICE RENDERED BY THE PERSONAL instruction Mrs. Wightman gave to scores of girls in the East," Bill Tilden said. Her prize eastern pupil was Sarah Palfrey, destined to become a historic champion, but a real puzzle to coach.

It was sometime in the fall of 1923 that the pro at the Longwood Cricket Club, a Mr. Croker, asked Hazel to take a look at an exceptional junior girl player from Boston. Croker could barely contain his enthusiasm over this prospect from a large wealthy family.

This was music to Hazel's ears, for she was becoming the first coast-to-coast tennis talent scout, although purely as a labor of love. Her motives were simply to identify talent and develop it for the sake of the game, and for women's tennis, and for the well-being of the individual. There were a few boys she encouraged along the way, but it was essentially her goal to assist, counsel, and support the nation's leading female talent in any way she could, in whatever stage of development she found it. She had just discovered Helen Jacobs in Berkeley a few months earlier. That same year her other prodigy, Helen Wills, won the first of her seven U.S. women's singles championships.

The East Coast at the turn of the century had never really had a good home-grown prospect to challenge the several ladies from Southern California, led by May Sutton, and those from Northern California, led by Hazel. This was a regional embarrassment to the East and an omission noticed publicly by Bill Tilden.

Star search missions have always been commonplace, but professionalizing the sport in modern times has made them more intense, and far less altruistic. Scampering pro agents and battalions of well-paid teaching pros are in the business of identifying, training, and promoting talent as quickly as humanly possible. Turning pro has meant in some cases that a child can then sign endorsement contracts and become an instant millionaire, as happened to Jennifer Capriati when she was thirteen. The far-flung grassroots programs of the predominantly amateur-based United States Tennis Association are also in the hunt as a part of its aim to "grow" tennis. All of this effort is connected in one way or another to the dollar-driven tennis industry. Hazel's thought was never complicated by money: she just wanted the individual to develop to be all he or she could be. It was for health and well-being, and for fun.

The girl she was asked to evaluate in 1923 was one of the older of the five tennis-playing Palfrey sisters. Casting her eyes over the lot of them hitting balls on Longwood's grass courts, Hazel agreed immediately that one did seem to have exceptional talent. But not the one Croker thought. It was the youngest, Sarah, who caught her eye. "I first saw Sarah when she was eleven years old and I marveled then at her perfect rhythm and timing. I have never seen her equal since," Hazel wrote in 1933, and given what she had seen, it was quite a sweeping remark.

"There were six of us Palfreys (five girls and a boy), and all of us loved tennis," Sarah Palfrey Danzig said in a 1991 interview. "We lived near the Longwood Cricket Club and many tournaments were held there, including the National doubles championships.

"And there were club championships and other tournaments all around the region—at the Essex Country Club the Agawam Hunt Club in Rhode Island and The Country Club. The latter was the first club in the United States; it never acquired any addition to the name. Mrs. Wightman helped supervise in all these tournaments and played in many. She went everywhere. She was already becoming a legend in her own club."

Hazel immediately took Sarah Palfrey under her wing, as well as all her sisters. All went on to win at least one national junior title. Sarah, however, beautiful, graceful, small at five feet three inches, and more delicate than muscular, went on to become a major international star. Despite a perplexing problem of nerves that hampered her for years, she compiled a significant record. Palfrey became the nation's leading junior player and went on to win thirty-nine junior and adult national titles. In a career abbreviated by a World War II tournament hiatus, she won the U.S. women's championships in 1941 and 1945, and the doubles nine times. In one stretch that included two Wimbledon crowns, she and Alice Marble (of San Francisco) didn't lose a doubles match in four years.

"We were very fortunate to have Mrs. Wightman as our mentor," Sarah said. "Everyone loved and admired her. She introduced us to all the top women and men tennis players of the day who came to Longwood—Helen Wills, Mary K. Browne, Bill Tilden, Billy Johnston, the great Australians, the four French Musketeers, and on and on through the years. We learned so much and were thrilled. But she coached and played tennis with any junior who was interested, and she often gave them a little red box of Sunmaid seedless raisins."

According to Palfrey, every time she stepped on the court with Mrs. Wightman it was a learning experience—exciting, fun, an exhilaration that was still, decades later, very real to her. In practice they often just volleyed point blank at each other across the net, loving the quickness of it and the challenge not to miss, until their arms got too tired to continue.

"It was she who taught me to love volleying," Palfrey said. "I couldn't help from the beginning absorbing her enthusiasm, imitating her style, and trying to learn some of her tricks.

"She was short physically and had to be amazingly quick with great anticipation. I think lots of the qualities rubbed off on me since I wasn't much taller than she was. And we got along beautifully. She could get back so quickly even for the deepest lobs because of her speed." Palfrey, who has hip problems from osteoporosis, was sitting on large cushions in her Manhattan apartment near Central Park. "I can still hear those feet rustling around. Soon, she asked me to be her doubles partner in some tournaments and exhibitions."

Mrs. Wightman invited Sarah to be her partner in the Women's Indoor Nationals in 1928. Sarah was fifteen. Mrs. Wightman was forty-one. It seemed a good way to help "season" the girl in adult competition and was similar to the way Hazel had assisted Helen Wills's career—by testing the deep waters early.

They won the title that year and the next three. In fact, the youngster would go on to make a significant reputation as a doubles player, winning the U.S. Championships nine times with four different partners. Practice for them was a thing of beauty, not of drudgery, whether at the club or at the Palfrey's summer place in Sharon, Massachusetts, where the girls maintained the private clay court by watering, rolling, and lining it.

"She was never bossy," Palfrey said. "She'd make suggestions like 'Sarah, don't forget the net's three feet high'—you know, humorous things like that. She didn't go into how to hit ground strokes, not like taking lessons from anyone. I probably should have spent more time with the ground strokes. But she'd tell me about strategy and tactics and where to put the ball. We'd often have luncheons and she'd talk about these things with people passing by, or we'd talk about them by ourselves. I loved being with her."

People often asked Mrs. Wightman to run tournaments and to give exhibitions at schools, colleges, and parks. She never turned any down. Palfrey remembers trips to Wellesley, Radcliffe, and Smith in Mrs. Wightman's red Cadillac. The students were most appreciative and showed their curiosity in the range of questions afterward.

"Of all of it, the Wightman Cup was the high point of my relationship with Mrs. Wightman. It was the result of all that had gone into it before, all the practice, all the playing. It seemed to bring out the best in people.

"I'll never forget my first Wightman Cup trip to Great Britain as a member of the team in 1930. Even though I got a state of nerves on Wimbledon's center court and lost my match, it was a great experience. I was seventeen and had been selected to play the third position on the team representing the United States against Great Britain. For the first time something really impressive was demanded of me. But my game wasn't equal to the demand and I found myself completely out of my depth. The match was over very quickly but the shattering effect on my nerves lasted for several years."

It was strange how assigning a daunting task at an early age had worked with one girl, Helen Wills, but not with another. For Palfrey the defeat at Wimbledon was a nightmare come true. The worst part was that the trauma stayed in her mind to hound her and affect her game. It later became the subject of an article she wrote for the *Atlantic Monthly*. At the time, Hazel offered aid and comfort, thinking it was a match to chalk up to experience.

"Mrs. Wightman was most understanding, though. She said nerves happen to many, many people, and that I shouldn't be disappointed because she wasn't.

"I went on playing on the Wightman Cup team for the next nine years, up until the war. My game and my nerves improved considerably and I won some good matches with the United States."

Palfrey snapped out of a growing habit of missing easy balls when she realized her nerves were only that, nothing more, and that she needed to work more on her ground strokes to gain additional confidence. After she did that, she won major singles titles. Nerves weren't particularly a problem when she played doubles because she had a supporting partner, and her concentration was steady.

"After the war we moved to New York, so I didn't see too much of Mrs. Wightman. But we kept in touch by mail and telephone. The last time I saw her in person was 1965 at Forest Hills, where they had a fashion show on center court.

"Mrs. Wightman was the guest of honor and she wore an exact reproduction of the dress her mother sewed for her in the early 1900s."

Sarah Palfrey Danzig was inducted into the International Tennis Hall of Fame at Newport in 1963, six years after Hazel. She died in 1996.

Chapter 8

LADY HOUSEGUESTS, WEST VISITS EAST

HAZEL WAS A PERIPATETIC TENNIS AUTHORITY WITH A SINGLE-HANDED MISSION to grow the game in America, and people everywhere listened to her. Bill Tilden said there was no one like her, male or female, in the sport.

By 1931, Tilden had stepped down as the world's number one amateur, ending his ten-year nonpareil reign, and he was pretty much finished barnstorming with the short-lived, financially chaotic little pro tour he had put together and starred in.

Tilden was a major analytic and critical voice in his time, and he was full of praise for Hazel. He was quoted in a newspaper as saying she was "the greatest asset to tennis in the country." The proof was "the number of nationally ranked girls from Boston." There were no high-ranking men from that area. "That's because there's no man with the experience, ability, and personality of Mrs. Wightman to aid the young boys," Tilden said. "Boston and the Pacific Coast," the Philadelphian declared, "are the greatest tennis centers in America."

By 1929, Wills ranked number one in the nation among women, Jacobs number two, and Palfrey, age seventeen, was number four.

Hazel's was the ultimate volunteer outreach. It had no exact date of origin. The free group lessons she extended to kids in the neighborhood and the greater Boston area, and any others who managed to show up for them, just grew from small seeds. In 1923, though, she started a winter Saturday indoor class on the chilly linoleum floors of the Longwood Covered Courts Club. The building, a low-slung architecturally graceless edifice that looked like a misplaced hangar, was just off the grounds of the Cricket Club. It provided a tennis fix for players who couldn't bear the thought of a cold turkey, tennis-less winter. Unlike the Cricket Club, it was open to the public. It was also the site of the national indoor doubles championships, which Hazel won ten times with three different understudies (Marion Zinderstein Jessup, Sarah Palfrey, and Pauline Betz), spanning the years from 1919 to 1941, when she was fifty-four. Building champions was not Hazel's prime goal. Spreading tennis was. Second was nurturing players, great and small. Sometime during these years she began to open her home as a sorority house for the elite girls and women of American tennis. Her home became a mission, a sanctuary, the venerated lodge of champions, with Hazel presiding as Queen Mother.

The height of her largesse was during the National Doubles at Longwood, when she entertained literally a packed house. The tournament was a fixture at Longwood from 1917 to 1969, the women moving to that venue in 1935. It had a cheery, competitive atmosphere all its own that pleased spectators and players alike. The club was steeped in history. The Davis Cup had begun there, and the father of the United States Tennis Association, James Dwight, was a member, as was Dick Sears, the first and seven-time winner of the national men's singles. Players were treated splendidly. Free housing was provided by the club members and the week was chock-full of social activities.

The crowds consisted of true fans filling the temporary stands to their capacity of two thousand. No one could fail to notice what *New York Times* sports writer Allison Danzig had observed about the event. "The competition was not grim," Danzig wrote. "There was a festive and friendly attitude there." For the finals of the nation's premier doubles event, the ticket line was often several hundred yards long.

Probably the earliest visitors in the evolution of Hazel Wightman's hospitality had been teenager Helen Wills and her mother in 1921, and then Helen Jacobs and her mother, and so on until the welcome mat was legendary worldwide.

In Herbert Warren Wind's piece on Hazel in *The Fireside Book of Tennis*, the writer for *The New Yorker* says that originally Hazel wanted to be a bridge for the top youngsters from California traveling to the East. For them, thousands of miles away from home by slow train, the pressures could be an intimidating experience. Often, even if the state association was willing to pay their expenses east to play in national tournaments, some wouldn't go because they had no connections in the East. While visiting in California, Hazel made it known that the girls would be welcome to make their headquarters at her house at No. 3 Charles Street in Brookline.

"An ever-increasing number accepted," Wind wrote. "In July and August when the young Californians moved in with their several rackets and changes of bandeaux, the yellow frame house on Charles Street seethed with the coloratura hum of a girls' dormitory as their housemother gave them careful instructions on what tournaments to enter, how to line up partners, where to stay on the circuit stops, what clothes to wear, how much to tip waiters, what evening invitations were preferable, and last but not least, how to improve their tennis."

To contemporary freewheeling teenagers, such care may sound like micromanaging and overprotection, but in those gentler days of manners and proprieties, it was a godsend. This avalanche of goodness coming freely from a woman who was a legend in her time was the apex of a tennis experience, too. It's not surprising that hundreds of people, especially senior women who are still steadfastly competing in their national tournaments, are devoted to her memory.

When in 1935 the Longwood Cricket Club became the dual site of the men's and women's national doubles championships (except for a stint at Forest Hills during the war years, 1942–1945), Hazel helped run it. Her duties did not impair her hospitality, however.

Indeed, after 1940, the guest numbers grew. After her divorce, Hazel moved that year into a larger house in Chestnut Hill behind the Cricket Club. The house was part of the settlement. The children were grown up and gone for the most part, but the two youngest, Dorothy, eighteen, and William, fifteen, were still at home.

Soon, during certain times of the playing season, even the best players from Australia, Brazil, England, and France, along with the Americans, were staying with Mrs. Wightman and her live-in combination cook and maid.

Some of them, especially foreigners, took it for granted they were to stay without being formally invited. Hazel came home one evening to find, to her surprise, Grand Slam winner Margaret Smith Court unpacked and sleeping in one of the upstairs rooms. Such faux pas might have tried her patience at times, but she was never offended. Nor did she ever turn anyone away, even if it meant taking extra measures. The maximum she hosted at one time was about eighteen. That meant putting up cots on the closed-in porch and in the basement.

Often appearing in sports magazines and Boston newspapers were picture spreads of the world's greatest women players, shown primly seated around Mrs. Wightman's huge oval dining room table at dinner and relaxing around the house.

For some, staying with Mrs. Wightie—a nickname that came out of the house in the 1930s— was an economic boon that helped ease the burden on the worldwide tournament trail. Shirley Fry from Akron was one such player. Her father supported her tennis wholeheartedly, but his was a large family of modest income. Fry won the national eighteens three years in a row and later became half of a top women's doubles team with Doris Hart, winning Wimbledon three times.

A wholesome, round-faced chatty girl whom everyone liked, Shirley always had to travel on the cheap. In an interview in his 1985 book, *Once a Champion*, she told author Stan Hart how it was in the Depression days of 1937:

"At first when I was a kid, I went with a dollar a day. That was all my parents, who were not well off, could afford. That paid for breakfast and dinner. We [the players] always stayed in people's houses—both the boys and girls. I remember when I was ten when my father sent me off from Akron to Philadelphia for a tournament. From Philadelphia, once the tournament was over, I took the train up to New York City, changed over to the subway—by now it is midnight—and went on to Forest Hills, where I stayed at the old Forest Hills Inn. I saw the matches there and went to the World's Fair at Flushing Meadows and came home. All alone. That was part of our training, all the children." Fry was another in the line of champions Hazel took in who benefited from her friendship and open-door policy.

Actually, during the third week of August in 1950, when the National

Doubles were played at Longwood, there was one group that Hazel did turn away. But it was only family. Her nephew Jim Hotchkiss remembers with some amusement dropping in on his Aunt Hazel with his family about that time. Hazel, who had put all her lessons on hold, was very apologetic in explaining the transformation the rambling brown-shingled house at 17 Suffolk Road would momentarily undergo. She took the time to give him a tour of the house nevertheless. "And here is normally where you would be staying any other time," he remembers her saying as she opened the door to a large upstairs bedroom, then adding reverentially, "but it's for Brough and duPont." Hotchkiss did not know Louise Brough and Margaret Osborne duPont from Abbott and Costello, but they were, of course, the greatest women's tennis team then the sport had known. The team won the U.S. Championships twelve times, a fact Hotchkiss learned soon afterward. His family stayed in a hotel.

No writer has captured the spirit and atmosphere of the house during that annual national convergence at Longwood better than the descriptive Mr. Wind. In *The Fireside Book of Tennis* he reports:

"During the tournament week, Mrs. Wightman rises at six o'clock, a half hour earlier than usual. While her housekeeper, Mollie Lennon, squeezes the orange juice for fourteen or more breakfasts, Mrs. Wightman, after raking the leaves from her lawn and checking her garden, jumps in her Studebaker and collects the day's provisions. On her return, she stations herself at the frying pan until the last breakfasters, invariably Brough and duPont, have been fed and packed off to their matches. Lunch is staggered, the girls returning to Suffolk Road whenever their schedules allow. Dinner is communal and vocal. After it is over, Mrs. Wightman, who plays in the veterans' division and runs the women's part of the doubles, relaxes over a cool Bendix washing machine in a basement alcove. She regards the Bendix as a touchy instrument that needs an experienced operator, and there is an unwritten law that while guests may iron their clothes, nobody washes except Mrs. Wightman. Around eight o'clock Chestnut Hill neighbors, male competitors, old Longwood hands, boyfriends, and star-struck pupils start to drop in, and for the next hour or so the decibel level (often helped along by Mrs. Wightman's strenuous piano work on "The Maple Leaf Rag") and the floor load of the house go up enormously. When the traffic has returned to normal, Mrs. Wightman is ready for a nice long tennis talk. To make certain that she doesn't loll around unorganized at any time during the day, Mrs. Wightman scratches memos to herself on a blackboard in the pantry and so is able to remember to drive to St. Joseph's Cemetery and water the flowers on Mrs. Lennon's husband's grave, to bake two batches of brownies and Toll House cookies daily, and to write and dispatch a dozen or so postcards, a supply of which she carries in her purse. . . ." A grand dame of Boston yes, but hardly the idle rich.

Many of the women who visited Hazel as California girls, or who were individually under her tutelage in the East, have continued playing competitively well into their sixties and seventies. The age competitions among women exist because Hazel was the guiding force behind the creation of the women's over-forty Grass Court Nationals in 1938, the initial senior women's event. Hazel herself never won the singles but took the doubles title eleven times with four different partners. Using five-year increments to determine a division, the United States Tennis Association added many more age groups, the bulk in the 1970s. Now it is a completely comprehensive system, with national tournaments played on four different court surfaces. In 1991, the seventy-fives and eighties divisions were added, and in 1995 a men's eighty-fives.

"We couldn't have played back then if it wasn't for Hazel," said Pat Yeomans of Los Angeles on a balmy afternoon in September 1990, reminding a luncheon group of women tournament players of their debt to the great lady. Yeomans, a historian of Southern California tennis, was helping direct the USTA Women's 70's Hard Court Championships at the Los Angeles Tennis Club. In the draw of twenty, eleven were from California, four from Texas, and one each from Florida, Colorado, Indiana, Idaho, and Wisconsin.

Yeomans was national Girls 18's champion in 1935, the year Hazel took her under her wing. Later, during the national women's doubles at Longwood, Hazel found her a spot in a boarding house across the street and arranged her meals, transportation, and matches. Yeomans (nee Pat Henry) stayed with her in 1936 and 1937 during the College Girls Invitational, which Hazel organized and personally directed. "She was the instigator and backbone of women's senior tennis, too," Yeomans said, "a full tilt lady. Her life is an example and an inspiration to every woman tennis player I know."

A top tournament player all her life, Yeomans had created a buffet luncheon to glorify and perpetuate the histories of four major figures in American women's tennis: Hazel, Helen Wills, May Sutton, and May's daughter, the pert, affable queen of the seniors, Dodo Bundy Cheney, who was then and there seeking her phenomenal 201st national title. Yeomans stood before the players and luncheon guests on the porch of the stucco and red tile club that was the headquarters of America's best tennis in the 1940s and 1950s and lectured without notes. Dates and statistics rolled forth like in a television quiz game. "How many of you here stayed with Mrs. Wightman?" she asked. Six hands went up and the memories came tumbling out.

Helen McDowell of West Los Angeles was a prime beneficiary of the veterans' tournaments. People told her she was too old to learn tennis in 1958 at the age of thirty-six. But she did and found a new world. "Dodo taught me, but Hazel told me when I played at Longwood never to hit a ball without a goal in mind. I will always remember that."

Marion Read, the number two ranking woman in the 70's division, said Hazel never knew half the behind-the-scenes tribulations the girls had trying to help out as guests at her home. Read, a woman of accomplishment, as many of the competitive women are, said one night the girls wanted to surprise Mrs. Wightie with a lobster dinner. Nancy Norton, a devoted product of Hazel's local group lessons, who volunteered domestic assistance in her college years and went on to become a history professor and dean, was part of the ad hoc culinary team. Just as the water boiled, the live creatures got free and began to roam the floor, their menacing claws trying to grope anyone entering the kitchen, inevitably causing seismic shrieking. "I was mortified," Read, a veteran of three major Himalayan expeditions, said. "But I said [to Nancy], I'll catch 'em if you'll put 'em in." And yet another doubles team clicked in a crisis. "Hazel never knew all the trouble we had," she added with a laugh.

The national doubles championships were a major event on America's tennis calendar and something the local newspapers did not ignore. Hazel apparently knew how to play the media's rather sexist game—to photographers, girls meant legs—while applying conventional taste and good sense. It was a clever union, and Hazel got women's tennis smack in the middle of the male-dominated sports pages.

Bud Collins, the flamboyant announcer who covers Wimbledon for NBC television and writes for the *Boston Globe*, explains the place Hazel occupied in the stream of Boston's sports journalism quite well. Boston had quite a bit of tennis going on when Collins arrived there as a college student in the 1950s from Ohio. He got a copy boy job at the *Boston Herald* that turned into part-time then full-time sports writing.

"When nobody was thinking of tennis, I remember my sports editor sent me out to cover the Massachusetts Women's Championships at Longwood in 1955," Collins said in an interview. "It was the first event I ever covered, and I was still in college.

"I knew more about tennis than he thought I would. Most reporters he sent to cover tennis were very reluctant to do it because it was the lowest sport. He said, 'Now don't worry, go out and introduce yourself to Hazel Wightman and she'll introduce you around and take care of you. Make sure your terminology is correct and don't miss any story.'"

All the reporters had to cover some tennis, Collins said, and Hazel was the contact, the resident authority, the Boston beacon. "She kept it alive," he recalls. For example, when Florida's Karol Fageros raised eyebrows by wearing gold lamé panties under her short tennis dress in the 1950s, the standard operating procedure was to call Hazel Wightman for a reaction.

"She understood what was going to get into the newspaper, too," Collins continued. "My sports editor would always say to Russ Adams, 'Russ, go out to Hazel's when there's a tournament in town.' And she'd get the prettiest girls and have them lined up in some way. My sports editor was dead set against printing a picture of a male tennis player. He thought they were all fags. And he had very little patience with tennis—except for Hazel. She was very strait-laced, friendly but very proper, astute and a good sport, too. And he loved cheesecake. And Hazel knew what he wanted.

"Yeah, she had a special place in the hearts of Bostonians."

Chapter 9

HAZEL'S GARAGE

There's nothing about the small, brown-shingled garage on Suffolk Road in Chestnut Hill to draw attention. It's a non-insulated edifice with sturdy wooden walls, common lighting, a peaked roof, and a concrete floor. Occasionally an approaching car will cut its acceleration to a crawl, then, satisfied with what probably was a nostalgic glance into memories of things past, speed away.

The garage was Hazel Wightman's workshop. It's a shrine now to hundreds who labored there. It was for rich and poor, pale and hardy, fat and thin, all imbued with some measure of devotion to the elusive skills of tennis. Whether self-committed or spirited there by commanding mothers who knew what was good for them, they pounded pellet-like balls in shivering winters against the wall with cutoff rackets until the sweat broke and quelled their shivering. In the standstill heat of summer they thumped away, dreaming of stadium court glories—or maybe just of beating somebody they thought needed a comeuppance.

The youngest was four and most were girls. Girls were very much deprived of sports for most of Hazel's life, and it is no doubt a reason she felt her messianic urgency day in and day out. She awoke with the sun, ready to make the world a better place through tennis.

"Boys usually learn tennis easier than girls because they're used to playing with a ball," she told writer and Yale student Janice Kaplan in a 1974 interview for an article called "Foremothers." "All little girls should be given a ball or a small racket or a bat. Some parents wait until a girl is twelve and then give her tennis lessons. Of course she'll be uncoordinated."

The origin of Hazel's love was first the ball itself and the wonderfully entertaining, absorbing things a human could do with one. Next was the racket and the control one could learn over the ball with it, the feel of that union coursing through the body, the soaring exhilaration of mastery—after mentally imprinting the obstacles of lines and net, or wall, or target. She didn't care for golf because it was too slow. She liked anything with a racket, except paddle tennis. "I don't like the sound of the racket, it's so dead," she said.

It wasn't just girls she taught or encouraged. Arthur Ashe, as a young visiting admirer, took his share of practice in the cramped footage of the garage that Mrs. Wightman had only slightly altered for against-the-wall bashing. She had covered the windows with plywood and the lightbulbs with chicken wire and had cleverly sloped the lower part of one wall so the bounce back would add a little loft to the ball.

"Naw, there wasn't much room in there," says Bud Collins, who came to know her well over the years. "You had to volley in self-defense. But anyone who came to her and asked, 'What am I doing wrong?' she would watch them and be happy to suggest things," he adds. "And she'd do that with good players. I think Frank Sedgman credited her with helping him at one time. And Gardnar Mulloy did. I know she was a friend of Arthur Ashe.

"She certainly encouraged a lot of people whose names we will never know, too. She was really a friend to anyone who wanted her advice. No one really was her equal in her contributions to tennis in the first half of the century."

Anyone making the pilgrimage to Suffolk Road, champion or duffer or family member, did not escape a tour of the garage, which is to say, a hit against its historic walls. Sometimes it was preceded with a bit of instruction. Hazel herself was a minimalist. With her classes, her attitude was, "If they're not told something else, they'll do it right themselves—like walking."

She never had a lesson herself, so she thought learning the stroke mechanics could come pretty naturally to someone with ball sense. The half-volley, one of the game's most demanding shots, was a snap for her. She recalled in her 1974 interview with *American Heritage*: "I had played two or three years when somebody said to me in Seattle, 'How'd you learn to make that half-volley?' And l said, 'What is a half-volley?' [That's] the truth. If somebody would have taught me, I never would have learned to make a half-volley, because they would have told me wrong."

Rhythm and balance were her watchwords. She demonstrated, then observed and barked terse instruction like an elfin drill sergeant. Be ready! Don't cross those feet! Get control!

"I always demonstrate with my own racket because people see easier than hear. Now, average teachers who are no good, I don't think they make an effort to explain properly, and of course rhythm is hard to explain. But most people who teach tennis don't feel the way I do about rhythm. I think the only way you can teach tennis is slow motion to begin with, so the ball is hit smoothly, rhythmically, nothing jerky about it."

Hazel saw most tennis teachers of her era as automatons lacking spirit, spark, and drive. She told *American Heritage* two weeks before she died in 1974, "Wherever I was, I used to teach. And in my garage . . . it's 'my' answer to teaching tennis. . . . You hit against the wall. The best wall, I think, is just wood. . . . A lot of people don't have the patience, but if more people used the bangboard, they would learn quicker. The garage—it's to me the perfect way of teaching and learning."

As one vexed family member once said after his sleek vehicle parked curbside had been generously adorned by the local birds, "Heaven forbid that anyone dropping by would ever think the garage was for cars!"

In 1933, seven years before the garage became her perfect tool, but with ten years teaching experience under her belt, Hazel wrote a book over several hours, days, and months of waiting while picking up the kids from school. She wrote it in longhand.

"It was put out by Houghton Mifflin, and of course they wanted a fancy book," she said. "When I looked at Billie Jean's book a few years ago, the first one she wrote, I tried to read it, but it was so technical. It was so difficult. If I were fifteen or sixteen, trying to learn tennis, I would have thrown it out the window. My book was plain, ordinary writing and plain, ordinary language, and it wasn't very pretty."

Parts of it read like a diary, such as this excerpt on "Teaching Children":

"Playing with children is its own reward. For years I have spent a great deal of my time coaching children and now and then running tournaments for them. In this activity I have been greatly aided by Mr. William S. Packer of Winchester, to whom I am greatly indebted, and whose help has encouraged me to attempt the children's tournaments as well as those for college girls in recent years. The work has been full of pleasure. At every successive visit to a school or playground, I see some result of my efforts that is gratifying. It may be evidenced only by the twinkle of an eye or a special smile from some shy child, or I may see an improvement in timing or anticipation. The field is infinite, and I make new discoveries continually. The naturalness of children and their response in unexpected ways give me endless enjoyment. My own tennis career, I strongly feel, would have been incomplete without this association with the younger generation."

A couple of years before the *American Heritage* interview, *Sports Illustrated* sent one of its hotshot writers out to watch Mrs. Wightie hold court in her natural habitat, the garage, and do a major story. The result was "The Original Little Old Lady in Tennis Shoes." In those days, Hazel was white-haired, still standing tall at five feet, and, at eighty-five, still tirelessly socking volleys against the wall for anyone to see. In running down her amazing volunteer record, including the fifty years of Red Cross help—from dishing ice cream to pouring coffee and serving donuts at 5 A.M. during two world wars—the writer quoted a Hazel watcher as saying the famous LOL had a "hopelessly grooved zeal for helping her neighbor."

"As the years have gone by," the *Sports Illustrated* writer wrote, "this zeal has manifested itself as a positive passion for teaching. . . . Her record might well make her the most successful instructor in the history of American tennis, and certainly the cheapest—she has never taken a cent."

How she was able to maintain such strength and stamina on the court at her advanced age is anybody's guess. It could never have been predicted from her sickly origins as a child, when she was out of school more than she was in, until she started playing ball games on the Healdsburg farm.

"I don't know how she does it," Mrs. Edith Sullivan, a very close friend, said, as quoted in *The New Yorker*'s 1952 profile. "Two summers ago, on a real broiler of a day, I watched Hazel giving pointers to a group of about forty girls. She stayed on the court for seven solid hours. She didn't even stop for lunch.

Around two, I handed her a tuna fish sandwich and she ate it with one hand and kept right on playing with the other."

She couldn't stop doing things. She seemed compelled to be occupied mentally or physically or both.

Four years after interviewing Hazel at eighty-seven, magazine writer Janice Kaplan wrote a reminiscence of that day for *Sports Illustrated*. Upon finding out that Kaplan was a sometimes player, Hazel had the college girl find a couple of rackets in the closet and help her lace on a pair of sneakers. Then the two walked down to the garage, the little old lady hobbling along with a crutch in one hand and a cane and racket in the other. Inside, she dropped away her crutch and cane and began slowly, a bit on the wobbly side, then steadied as an infusion of new vitality took over, bringing a shine to her eyes and crispness to her voice.

"It's so easy!" she exclaimed. "I can hit the ball a thousand times and never miss! Here," she said suddenly, "let's play a game."

And so the two played, Hazel missing nothing that she could get a racket on, reproaching the Kaplan girl for her unnatural swing, chattering commands, getting into it in a way that so impressed and transfixed Kaplan that she lost track of time. "I'm glad we played," Hazel said after what could have been as much as an hour of this. "I've gotten too lazy lately. You have to keep active to be happy."

Back at the house then, she sank into a big chair and frailty again took her over. It could well have been her last garage trip, for not long afterward she was confined to a wheelchair and then died that December, shortly before her eighty-eighth birthday.

Her book, long since out of print, is a green, hardbound ninety-three-page volume of her feelings about "better tennis" and how to attain it. At the end, like a postscript, there's an attempt to shrink her wisdom. Ever anxious to simplify and make the game digestible and fun, she has a two-and-a-half-page list of "Points to Remember" followed by a single page of "Slogans and Maxims." If readers find this nonetheless too wordy, Hazel boils it all down to far less than a page called "A Tennis Alphabet":

>**A**lways Alert
>**B**e Better
>**C**oncentrate Constantly

Don't Dally
Ever Earnest
Fair Feeling
Get Going
Hit Hard
Imitate Instructor
Just Jump
Keep Keen
Less Loafing
Move Meaningly
Never Net
Only Over
Praise Partner
Quash Qualms
Relax Rightly
Stand Straight
Take Time
Umpire Usually (on request)
Vary Volleys
Work Wiles
Xceed Xpectations
Yell Yours
Zip Zip

At first glance it's an amusing, quirky style out of antiquity. But for all of that, it may well work. It's a valid test to ask what Hazel meant by each expression, for each bore a lesson. And each is easy to remember in the heat of battle when a player, alone, is his or her own natural coach.

How indelible any of her words became is guesswork, as is the number of children she taught. But people who have an idea, like teaching pro Bill Drake, are impressed. The coach of former touring pros Barbara Potter and Tim Mayotte, Drake is employed by The Country Club, a spacious old private club in Brookline. Long before Drake arrived there, Hazel had been a formidable regular at the bridge tables in the large, wooden, vibrant yellow clubhouse. Today, the grounds have many modern recreational facilities, even an indoor court where Drake was teaching one day.

"Hazel Wightman?" he said, poking his head out the door. "Just about every day I run into her legacy. I've been a pro in New England more than twenty years—twelve years here—and I've experienced this as a teacher. I run into people all the time who were taught by her. And they have beautiful games. It must be in the thousands. It's just amazing."

Chapter 10

TEACHING THE ENGLISH, THE EVOLVING WIGHTMAN CUP

THE 1946 WIGHTMAN CUP MATCHES WERE WITHOUT COMPARISON—HISTORIC, nostalgic, abysmally lopsided and sad. But the circumstances after a devastating world war were so unusual that they could not serve as a bellwether for the future of the Wightman Cup. There was hope.

With the exception of the U.S. Championships, all major competition had ceased from 1940–1945 while the Allied Powers of the free world fought the aggression of Germany and Japan. Now it was time to get back to work and rebuild and restore the wonderful things that made life worth living. People desperately wanted the amateur sport to return to its glorified past. They longed for the great players to again link arms across the seas, to be seen in all the old familiar places, to thrill the steadfast fans.

There was a reunion of former U.S. Wightman Cup members at Forest Hills before the 1946 team flew over to Wimbledon. It was the first flight for all of them, and emblematic of the postwar revolution in passenger transportation. So used to taking many suitcases with them and being pampered by porters, the women arriving at the airport looked like they were packing away an opera company and proved to be grossly overweight. Margaret Osborne's boyfriend had, as a gift, ordered expensive and unusual wooden racket holders for each team member. These large, elaborate racket presses held six frames and guarded against warping. But they were so heavy they were the first thing jettisoned.

Pan American's "New York" Clipper left La Guardia at 4 P.M. on its inaugural transatlantic flight to London (Heathrow) Airport. Not wanting anyone's hands to be idle on the interminable flight, Hazel brought her needlepoint and taught the team the craft so they wouldn't be bored. The Clipper arrived at 5 A.M. New York time, or 10 A.M. London time, smack in the midst of a blustery rainstorm.

Because the historic arrival was a media event, so many tents were set up at the airport it looked like the team had flown into a circus. NBC television was there to broadcast live. But there were few TV sets in America because people considered the pricey newfangled contraptions not yet trustworthy.

As soon as Hazel stepped out of the plane she, as non-playing captain, was whisked into a tent to be interviewed by the BBC as the nasty storm pelted the airport. She was proud of this team that had dominated the U.S. nationals during the war years, she said. It consisted of Pauline Betz, Louise Brough, Margaret Osborne, and Doris Hart. And they would go on to dominate the 1946 Wimbledon, too.

Osborne, now Margaret duPont, remembers how crippled the country was. "There was no food in England then," she says. "Things were in shambles. At the All-England Club Stadium there was a gaping hole where a German bomb had fallen and wiped out twenty-three hundred seats." America's leading male player, Jack Kramer, had some influence in the meat-packing industry, and carried over a two-week supply of steaks on his flight.

Louise Brough, now Louise Clapp, recalls the reception in the tent "with lots of sandwiches but few sweets. There was a sugar shortage, you know. We stayed at the Dorchester Hotel, a luxury hotel, but it didn't have much food."

Brough and Osborne went on to become the greatest women's doubles team in history. Playing individually in singles or as a doubles team, they compiled an unsurpassed Wightman Cup record over many years. They were never defeated. Margaret Osborne duPont served as captain for nine different teams.

"We always dressed alike and had, oh, six or seven costumes that matched," Brough says, then adds with a laugh, "Ted Tinling [the late British dressmaker] said we looked like nurses! But I remember that week in 1946 vividly. Every morning Mrs. Wightman got up early and went off to teach clinics at schools and then would rush back to us. She was busy all the time."

Brough's connection to Mrs. Wightman went back to her junior days when she and her mother would stay at the Wightman house. "She was particularly nice to me," Brough says. "Maybe it was because I always straightened out her cabinets and lined up the glasses just so. She said I was a tidy person to have around. But really, it was just one big happy family being there."

Typical of her thoroughness and her sense of global community, Hazel had written ahead to the Red Cross and had managed to get its London office some Wimbledon tickets. Delighted, Red Cross officials naturally offered her any conceivable assistance that could make her sojourn easier. It so happened that the girls had neglected to bring any wool socks, the best possible footwear. "There is no such thing as a woman's wool sock to be found in Great Britain at the present moment" was the way William L. Gavin of the London office began in his June 17, 1946, letter responding to Hazel's request. The very next day, however, Gavin had become a miracle worker. He wrote: "I hand you herewith eighteen pairs of grey woollen socks which I very much hope will fulfill the girls' requirements." Hazel, who carried a letter of introduction from American Red Cross official Harvey Gibson, definitely knew how to work things. Moreover, she got the whole team meal tickets at the U.S. Commissary through the connections of the duPont family.

The Duchess of Kent attended the matches. The Queen Mother came once, too. As Her Highness was being seated, this august event was enough to cause Pauline Betz, on court, to tremble. Once she felt she had collected herself, Betz then resumed play with a double fault.

As it was, warmed by the socks or otherwise inspired, the Americans, who had dominated the series 13-4 before the war, trounced the British seven matches to zero without the loss of a set. It was the worst beating the U.S. had administered since the origin of the cup in 1923. Only one set in the seven matches went to extra games.

It was a sad showing from the brave country that had been torn apart by the terrifying Luftwaffe night shellings, while our tranquil shores had remained unpenetrated by foreign enemies. Sports throughout England were much diminished. "There are no promising English youngsters in sight," declared Hazel, the First Lady of American tennis. "The war set English tennis back quite a few years. What it needs now is good coaching. The English coaches themselves must be stimulated."

She decided she was the person to do it. Made an honorary member of the All-England Club at Wimbledon that year, and twice presented to the queen, Hazel stayed in the war-ravaged country six weeks. She traveled around London and the countryside giving clinics at schools and delivering her small, unassuming speeches. Rounding out her design was a plan to make a four-hundred-foot movie short of the U.S. women players at the August national doubles tournament in Longwood. It was to be a British training film. She would bear the cost of it herself.

Her Wightman Cup adventure of 1946 wasn't quite over, though. Her return flight was an air travel lesson she probably had nightmares about for years after. Her DC-4 flight with its fifty-five passengers was, after seventeen hours in the air, forced to land at Brainard Field in Hartford, Connecticut, because of low visibility at La Guardia in New York. Wrung out by the ordeal, and wishing to avoid any more misery, Hazel took a three-hour cab ride home, carrying the cup in her arms. She had had enough of airplanes.

In 1947, she sent the training film to England. The next year, her thirteenth and final time as Wightman Cup captain, she returned to England as a tennis celebrity, having taken the *Queen Elizabeth* luxury liner over.

Despite all of Hazel's efforts, the response from Britain on court, as reflected in match scores over the years, was weak. The United States beat the British twelve straight years after World War II. Seven were shutouts. Margaret Osborne duPont and Louise Brough remained the premier women's doubles team in the world, and if one was sick the other could play with just about anyone else and win. Broughie, as she was nicknamed, played nine years of singles and doubles and was never beaten in her twenty-two matches.

America had plenty of new stars coming up besides young Doris Hart, too. Shirley Fry was next, then Maureen Connolly, then the rangy serve and volley champion out of Harlem, Althea Gibson, the sport's first African-American champion, whom Hazel readily befriended.

A break in the dominating pattern showed up in 1958 with the appearance of two British girls, towering Christine Truman and the left-handed blonde Ann Haydon. Leading the Brits to victory that year, they continued to be a force until 1961, when Southern Californians Karen Hantze and Billie

Jean Moffitt, a gutsy sandlot baseball player as a kid, came along to win the cup easily that year and put the U.S. on a seven-year streak.

By the late 1960s, Great Britain had another world star to throw into its lineup. She was Virginia Wade, a college math and physics graduate and athletic daughter of an archdeacon. She ended up playing Wightman Cup for twenty-one years. Wade, along with Mrs. Ann Haydon Jones, the sisters Christine and Nell Truman, plus Sue Barker, kept things nicely competitive and winning in 1978. After that, American teams led by such players as Chris Evert Lloyd, Tracy Austin, Andrea Jaeger, Rosie Casals, Kathy Jordan and Martina Navratilova never again lost the cup as the British champions faded away and no one of their caliber replaced them. In 1990, the Wightman Cup was suspended.

Since open tennis began in 1968, players had been playing for money. That itself was not an easy transition for Wightman Cup competition to make. Backed by the two national associations and well attended by the public, the Wightman Cup was an amateur contest meant to foster international sportsmanship and goodwill. These were shining ideals of another era—one whose time had passed. Amateurism was the polar opposite of professionalism, and professionalism meant commercialism. It seems a quaint notion nowadays to say that playing the Wightman Cup was a reward for prominent women who played for the love of the game. They were selected by their countries to represent them as a team. It was fun, and an adventure. But with each passing year after 1968, it became a harder idea to sell to the top players, whose time could be measured in tournament or exhibition money. Players expected compensation. Britain and the U.S. soon had to come up with some sort of payment for the winning and losing team members. This significantly increased the cost of putting it on.

In the big picture, the Wightman Cup had a huge effect on the youth of America. Its popularity came about because over the years hundreds of Junior Wightman Cup teams had been formed throughout the nation for inter-club, intra-state, inter-state, and inter-regional competition. The best girls were delighted to be chosen. It was an honor. It meant travel and fun and meeting new people and playing in nice clubs. The USTA sections picked up the bills. This formed the backbone of girls' team play at the grassroots level in the U.S. And it was all organized by volunteers from the various USTA sections. The boys had a similar competition with Junior Davis Cup.

Wightman became a household word in tennis communities. The phrase "Wightman Cup" appeared on the sports pages across America every year. Possibly a snippet of the activities would show up in *Movietone News* or on *The March of Time* at movie theaters.

Hazel made her final appearance as playing captain of the team in 1931. She was captain twelve times, the last in 1948. Convinced she had served enough then, she asked Mrs. Marjorie Gladman Buck to succeed her.

In 1973, a little more than a year before Hazel died, the fiftieth anniversary of the cup (it wasn't played during WWII) was staged at her beloved Longwood Cricket Club. When told the plan was afoot, she said flatly she wouldn't come because she didn't feel like doing those things anymore. She changed her mind when the event arrived.

"I was there every day," she said in the *American Heritage* interview. "I didn't miss a thing. I even went to dinner at a backyard supper party. Oh, it couldn't have been a better thing. And they made up this beautiful program. [There] is a picture of me on the front, and pictures of teams, teams, teams, and very few beer ads, and very few whisky ads. . . ." The postwar photographs in the program are of women in short white skirts and white Wightman Cup blazers standing, sitting, walking toward the camera, clutching bouquets, touching the cup itself, and always smiling. They were special times for the players and had an exclusive international flavor in a time when tennis was not in the Olympics. Billie Jean King remembers how snazzy the Wightman Cup blazer looked, and the pride she felt wearing it while representing her country.

The fiftieth was more than a birthday party. It symbolized Hazel's triumph in international goodwill. Boston Mayor Kevin H. White proclaimed it "Mrs. Wightman Day" for the city. British writer Laurie Pignon, who covered the matches, reported the scene this way:

"No camera froze the tiny tear that squeezed its reluctant way from the corner of her eye; it was her secret as she stood in the middle of the centre court at the Longwood Cricket Club as a thunder of cheers seemed to fill a cloudless world. 'It was the first time I cried in public,' Mrs. Hazel Hotchkiss Wightman later told me. But her tear wasn't alone. There were others more noticeable among the five thousand who had come to honor the First Lady in lawn tennis and the fiftieth anniversary of the cup she gave to the game."

After 1968, appealing to an invitee's patriotism was sounding more and more like a rather hollow plea. Even so, the Americans were so deep and strong on the world ranking computer that regardless of who was finally recruited, the overall match result was predictable. The last year of competition, 1989, America's thirteen-year-old Jennifer Capriati, then unranked altogether, beat England's number three player, Clare Wood, 6-0, 6-0. The U.S won all matches without the loss of a set. As in 1946, however, one set did go into extra games.

Meanwhile, the International Tennis Federation had started the Federation Cup in 1963. This competition had the exact same worldwide intention as the Wightman Cup back in 1923, when only England showed up to play. But forty years later other nations were inclined to participate, especially Australia, which was developing depth behind its great star Margaret Smith. And two years after her first Wightman Cup appearance, Billie Jean King played on her first Federation Cup team, narrowly defeating Australia 2-1 in the final.

Ultimately, no sponsor could be found for the Wightman Cup, and the two national associations could not see the point of continuing. Suddenly, in the 1990s, all the years of flag-waving pomp and grandeur were gossamer memories, and the Wightman Cup was irrevocably obsolete.

A total of ninety-two American women played in Wightman Cup, and seventy-two British women. Chris Evert played thirteen years and was undefeated in twenty-six singles matches. Virginia Wade holds the record for the number of participating years, twenty-one, and she was captain of the British squad fourteen times.

The Wightman Cup became a living memory at the College of William and Mary in 1995. The college had been the playing site of the last four cup competitions in America, and the Wightman Cup has a permanent display on campus in the new McCormack-Nagelsen Tennis Center.

(Appendix A lists the ninety-two American players and their years and records)

Chapter 11

MODERN PLAYERS, MODERN COSTUMES

IN HER FIRST APPEARANCE IN THE NATIONAL WOMEN'S TOURNAMENT AT THE Philadelphia Cricket Club in 1909, Hazel had unintentionally shocked the staid audience by violating the unofficial dress code. Her dimity cotton, ankle-length dress was long enough. But it was those darn sleeves of hers. They were too short. Her bare forearms were showing! You can imagine the snide remarks. Was this the way of the Wild, Wild West? Had young western women no breeding? Why, it was the way a veterinarian delivered a foal!

Hazel couldn't stand to play tennis with more than that amount of material covering her short arms, and that was that. But of course every time a player showed up with something a little bit shorter, the audience stirred uneasily and tittered. Bare skin, or the hint of it, was scandalous, pure and simple. Men used to idle at popular intersections after a rain just to see women raise their skirts above the ankle to jump daintily over a puddle at the end of a boarded sidewalk. And there was a cute, popular song then entitled "They're Wearin' 'Em Shorter in Hawaii," a risqué little ditty that referred to skirts.

Progress in tennis dress, like the sport itself, was a game of inches. Headstrong May Sutton bared her wrists, Hazel her arms. Suzanne Lenglen wore "indecent" diaphanous skirts at Wimbledon. Helen Wills shed her long stockings.

"It was ridiculous," Hazel said, recalling the insufferable length of dresses in her 1970s interview with Janice Kaplan. "But I could never play in the short dresses the girls wear now. I'd be embarrassed to bend over. I love to watch the girls play—but I'd prefer not to see so much of their panties."

It seems amazing that Hazel Hotchkiss Wightman could, over seventy years of tennis, maintain the levelheadedness she did about the sport after the onslaught of radical changes in 1968. The dress code was just one such change. Professionalism was another. Teaching another.

Hazel died about eight years before wood rackets went the way of the car running board, and before the advent of oversized rackets made of synthetic fibers and wielded by increasingly larger women. It was odd. Tilden had noted in his book that Hazel's San Francisco friend, practice partner, and adviser Maurice "The California Comet" McLoughlin had revolutionized the game in 1909 with his powerful serve and his net-rushing, volleying, and smashing. "The god Speed was at the wheel," Tilden declared, himself the master of the "cannonball" serve. But it was nothing compared to what the top men and women do to the ball now. And a woman just five feet tall? Now, five feet six inches is considered short in the pro ranks. One hundred pounds is anemic.

Hazel was confident that at the height of her youth and form, she could have given the top modern players an anxious moment or two. But little else. She wouldn't have considered herself a threat to the champions of a later era, such as Martina Navratilova, Chris Evert, or Evonne Goolagong, let alone the stronger and taller champions, like Steffi Graf and Monica Seles, who replaced them.

"I couldn't beat those girls," she confessed to *American Heritage* magazine. "They are too fast . . . too agile. In a doubles game I would hold my own. My problem would be the distance. You see, I am too short to be able to cover the ground that these girls can who are eight inches taller than I am. They would be a whole stride ahead of me all the time." To say nothing of reach.

According to the late renowned tennis gadfly and dress designer Ted Tinling, originally of London, later of Philadelphia, the evolution of the abbreviated dress code trend included a distinct "masculine" look during the Great Depression. Tinling was one of the most observant and articulate social commentators the game has known, its solitary historian of style. A prewar designer of evening clothes and bridal wear, Tinling, a six foot- five-inch bald man with large ears and bulging eyes, was on the international scene in some sort of official role all his life. Most often it was with women's tennis, starting when he was a gawky, tennis-smitten thirteen-year-old. He was one of the few who vividly remembered seeing the ballyhooed Wills-Lenglen exhibition showdown on the French Riviera in 1926.

To historians who can remember the all-white tradition of attire, Tinling was the one who designed "gorgeous" Gussie Moran's lace panties, which so shocked the male-dominated All-England Club at Wimbledon in 1949. Newspapers, newsreels, and radio went crazy over it. The fetching Moran, a fairly good American player from Santa Monica, became an overnight sex symbol. In his memoirs, Tinling said that as a result of the "staggering" response, even "a racehorse, an aircraft, and a restaurant's special sauce were named after her."

Tinling was one of the few who ran afoul of Hazel at the height of her popularity—or perhaps Tinling would suggest her "powers," as the more apt description. Hazel did ride high. She had major influence and used it where she saw fit. She had earned it, after all.

What led up to Tinling's famous tiff with Hazel were some noteworthy historical moments. Alice Marble, the boyish champion who rolled her shoulders when she walked and angrily cussed and banged balls into the net when she lost a point, "spearheaded the era of masculinity," Tinling wrote. In the late '30s, she wore shorts, a shirt, and a white ball cap.

"It was carried over to the postwar years, when Louise Brough, Margaret Osborne, Pauline Betz, and Pat Todd arrived in the first plane to touch down in '46 at London's new Heathrow airport," Tinling wrote (mistaking Doris Hart for Todd). "The masculine look of the women players who came to prominence during the war years related to the regimentations of war, when it was unavoidable that unisex duties should lead to unisex clothes. One of the major factors in the explosive reaction to Gussy's panties was the conscious, and subconscious, revulsion against this masculinity that was still obvious in tennis even four years after the war had ended."

Factoring into this social equation somewhere would be the barracks popularity of the GI pinup girl, which produced the busty "Lana Turner era" of the late '40s. The postwar mainstream wanted its girls feminine. Girls playing tennis didn't want their movements restricted. Some were prudish, others weren't. So how would it work out?

Hardly a tennis dress was for sale in the U.S. or Great Britain then. It was all well-above-the-knee shorts or baggy culottes. Following Christian Dior's Paris "New Look—a return to femininity and sexual attraction—Tinling, back in London after serving as a British Army Intelligence officer for seven years, took it upon himself to fix tennis. He let his intentions be known, and one by one the British ladies commissioned him to design dresses for them. His resulting white, mid-thigh creations were smart, made all the more distinct by a thin line of color at the hemline. Tinling, who had the pleasant prewar task of escorting players from the dressing room door onto the stadium's centre court, was not aware of any rule against color, just that the tradition was all white, a subtlety he was prepared to explore. What amounted to hardly more than piping seemed innocuous enough.

His sky-blue or rose-pink line got a half inch thicker in 1948, beginning with Betty Hilton, a member of the British Wightman Cup team that year. For Hilton he even added a zigzag top line to the color. The debut of that dress was in the first Wightman Cup singles match at Wimbledon in 1948. And in the quickest defeat in cup history, Hilton lost the opener 6-1, 6-1 to the heavily favored American, Louise Brough. "Betty lost because she was self-conscious about the color on her dress!" Tinling wrote that Hazel said to him right afterward. He went on: "The next day I was shocked to hear that Hazel had asked the Wimbledon Committee to ban both Betty Hilton and Joy Gannon from wearing dresses I had designed for them.

"When I arrived at Wimbledon to carry out my Call-Boy duties, Hazel embraced me superficially and kissed me on both cheeks with the smug smile she used on people she had just beaten in a match. 'No hard feelings, of course,' she said. 'But we do play tennis in white, don't we?'"

Tinling said he had two reactions to this. He recalled Hazel had ordered Helen Jacobs not to wear shorts at Wightman Cup matches at Forest Hills in 1933 and sent her scrounging through her luggage to find a single soiled dress. This was two months after Jacobs had launched the novelty of shorts for women by appearing in them at the All-England championships, "and looking particularly good in them," in Tinling's opinion. The second thought was more esoteric. It was a historical flash of King Canute of England, an egotist who thought his power greater than the power of ocean waves. He tried to prove this to his courtiers by ordering them to carry him out on his royal seat into the white-capped surf, which he loudly commanded to cease. It didn't, of course, and the king and his hapless bearers almost drowned. "I told Hazel Wightman in 1948 that henceforth I would call her Queen Canute," Tinling said. "World frontiers had been changed, civilization had barely survived its greatest threat, but Hazel Wightman thought she could hold back the tide." For several years afterward the two frostily avoided each other, and not a word was spoken between them.

If Hazel felt her power it was because she had earned it and felt obliged to stand by certain traditional standards. It was probably enjoyable power, too. But invariably, somebody wouldn't like her style and interpretations, and a brouhaha like this only gained Tinling more attention, which he never shrank from. After a while even Hazel's stalwart supporters thought she was a bit pushy. This was her rigid period. "She could be very strait-laced in that time period after World War II," Bud Collins said. "But she had been the one to proclaim short sleeves. So it was sort of amusing."

Another person who ran afoul of her was Tom Stow of the Berkeley Tennis Club. Stow was the teaching pro, a brilliant pioneer in the field of mechanical analysis. Stow spent a good deal of time examining how golf was broken down and taught. An outstanding doubles player at UC Berkeley in the mid-'20s, Stow was one of the first to make a living as a bona fide teacher. He is credited with rigorously preparing Don Budge over several months to win the first Grand Slam in 1938. He also is credited with helping out two of Hazel's favorite understudies about then, Sarah Palfrey and Margaret Osborne duPont.

Sarah had been taught by Hazel but hadn't quite been able to climb the highest mountains. A major title must have been a very dear goal for the girl whose father was the executive lawyer for Oliver Wendell Holmes. A great success meant a kind of sweet adulation by the public, which was then closer to the stars. That and the trophy were the payoffs, not gobs of money. Sarah's husband, Elwood Cooke, suggested in 1940 she visit Stow. He was known for dismantling a stroke, then properly reconstructing it.

"He [Stow] helped me tremendously with my backhand when I stayed out in California for three months," Palfrey said in an interview. "I played almost every day with him. He changed my grip. It took me a whole year before I got used to it. And the following year was the first year I won the U.S. Championships. He helped my whole style become more aggressive."

One can only speculate over how the two teachers must have clashed in basic attitudes when Hazel visited the West: she, the consummate amateur and volunteer, giving away pearls of wisdom, worshipped high and low as the mother of tennis, and Stow, first the struggling, deeply committed pro, then a gray eminence with a dozen or more disciples, destined to be hailed in the West as a father of modern professional tennis teaching. The gap did not fully close in their lifetimes.

Another area of consternation was pro tennis. Hazel had the honor of handing out the first equal paycheck at the 1973 U.S. Open, twenty-five thousand dollars to Margaret Court. The trouble wasn't just the idea of playing for money. Hazel was adapting to that. Women, in fact, were advancing as they never had before. But it was the newfangled contexts and experimentations. They were so baffling, the old guard was reeling.

The height of this revolution was found in World Team Tennis, with teams of men and women playing short sets with no-ad scoring, and substituting allowed. It was like pro wrestling and almost as noisy, for in a historic affront, team tennis dashed the game's sacred politeness imperative and supplanted it with an audience's spontaneous, raucous bellowing. "Tro da bum out!" was an exclamation whose time had finally come in tennis, despite the discomfort it caused in just about every audience.

Hazel took it all in stride. "After the first match I saw, I was pretty sure I wasn't going to like it, because of the rowdyism," she said in 1974. "I am one of the few people that believe that the audience should be quiet when people are playing tennis. I remember the first time I ever gave a thought to it. I was playing against May Sutton, and the gallery had gotten so big because it made tennis popular to see two women playing, one from Northern California and one from Southern California, and they [the audience] were shouting, 'Come on, northern girl! Come on, southern girl!' It nearly killed me. I realized that the reason noise bothered me particularly is I depend on hearing the sound of the ball on the racket. The hearing is very important because when I hear the ball hit so loud, I know it's going to go farther. It may be hit so it's going to be a half-volley, it may be hit so it's going to be a high lob. I depend on hearing it." She had some other qualms, too. She thought the stress level was too hard on the girls.

Hazel had been opposed to team tennis from the outset and didn't think it would take hold. It didn't really. It died out for a few years but then was revived by Billie Jean King. King fervently believes in the concept and has been keeping a nationwide league alive. It's a one-month summer diversion from the circuit with retired stars such as Martina Navratilova and Jimmy Connors and John McEnroe, plus an assortment of players who couldn't make more money playing elsewhere.

Yet something about it intrigued Hazel. Maybe it was the old chemistry that first drew her to the sport in the first place—the rackets, the ball, the quickness, the teams and excitement. Forget garish colors, boorish crowds, even manners.

The first winter of team tennis in the early '70s, Hazel went to see the Boston Lobsters team play six times. Audiences, usually expected to be quiet and applaud at only appropriate times, were encouraged over the public address system to yell like they would at a baseball game. It reminded her of kids shouting when she was a youngster and climbed a ladder using only her hands, or pole-vaulted over a fence on a dare. Her intense feelings were characteristics that brought her closer in spirit to explosive Billie Jean King, one of the league's top players. Hazel had followed her career since King was a teenager on the Wightman Cup team. She loved Billie Jean's style of play but deplored her court outbursts; they drove her crazy, as Alice Marble's had. She gave Billie Jean major credit for leading the women's game into the professional era. Billie Jean respected Hazel, and the feeling was mutual. "Billie Jean is very interested in history and was thrilled to know Mrs. Wightman," Bud Collins said. "Billie Jean is her spiritual heir, I think."

Billie Jean Moffitt King had played on ten Wightman Cup teams and eight Federation Cup teams and was a spunky, outspoken leader of the World Team Tennis movement. An excellent doubles player with many Grand Slam titles, she was a team girl all the way. Probably her most fun-filled year was 1961, when she was seventeen and won the Wimbledon doubles with Karen Hantze, eighteen, and also played on her first Wightman Cup team. Bursting with youthful spirit, the underdog U.S. team dramatically upset England 6-1 at Chicago's Saddle and Cycle Club, and she was practically delirious over it.

"We were supposed to lose 7-0," King said in an interview. "They had Christine Truman and Ann Haydon (Jones). I remember Margaret Osborne was my captain and I was so glad she was there. I got one of those beautiful white blazers to wear—my parents still have a picture of me in it.

"They couldn't figure out how they lost to us. They were in a stupor. We got headlines in the *Tribune* and I was thrilled. We were all just like little kids celebrating."

King first met Hazel Wightman that year at Longwood during the U.S. National Doubles tournament. King never did stay with Mrs. Wightman, mainly because the tournament set her up with private housing elsewhere.

"I had read all the history I could get my hands on," King said. "I was just into it, and I knew everything about her. She was tiny and forthright. Used understatement. And to play as well as she had in her life, she had to have been very agile.

"I liked her because we liked the same things."

When she was still a major force on the women's pro tour, King, then twenty-nine, faced Bobby Riggs in 1973 in the Battle of the Sexes, a one hundred-thousand-dollar winner-take-all exhibition. It was the biggest single cash prize ever offered in tennis.

This was a production of absurd hoopla, and Hazel was swept into the frenzy that raced over America. Riggs, fifty-five, was a court hustler and consummate gambler who had nonetheless been a solid champion. He won a Wimbledon triple in 1939 and because of bets he placed on himself to sweep all the titles, he walked away with about a hundred thousand dollars. He later played on a barn-storming pro tour. Generally known as a chatty character willing to wager on anything, he was rather well liked by his peers. Stories about him abound. He was notorious for setting up handicapped matches with rich guys in Florida. Playing for a hundred dollars a set, say, Riggs might don raincoat and galoshes while carrying an empty bucket in his left hand.

As a joke, Riggs had cajoled shy superstar Margaret Smith Court into playing him for winner-take-all money on Mother's Day earlier that year. Court's nerves weren't quite up to it. Riggs trounced her and got a small beam of media light for it. Then a public exchange of sexist comments with lippy and eager Billie Jean King ensued and grew over several weeks, this at the height of the Women's Liberation Movement. Ultimately, Riggs's flinging down of the gauntlet to Billie Jean led to the showdown at the Houston Astrodome on September 20, 1973.

The Battle of the Sexes was the most publicized sporting event in tennis history. Even janitors stopped work to watch televisions that night. It was like no other encounter before or since: a top woman pro playing a cocky, aging former men's pro who had been bragging about how vastly superior men were to women on the court.

Experiencing the showdown live were 30,472 spectators. More than fifty million viewers watched the best of five set match on television. Sexism was on stage, and the media had a field day. King won in straight sets rather handily, and women's tennis got a shot in the arm that never wore off.

"Nobody enjoyed it more than I," Hazel said a few months later, the same year she died. "Bud Collins had sent a car to take me over to his studio to talk about it. So whatever he asked me I answered. I must have sounded awfully stupid. He said who did I think was going to win. At that time I'd seen Margaret Court play Riggs and I'd seen Billie Jean never rise to any great occasion by that time; and whereas I wanted her to win like nothing at all—I'd have given anything in the world to have her win—I couldn't say I thought she would. And yet when she got to playing good tennis that night, outplaying Bobby, no one was happier than I.

"Oh, I was so proud of her. I was so *proud* of her, and as a matter of fact, you know, I watched her lips, and I don't think she swore once. And that was the first time I've ever been so pleased with her. I was so pleased that I could be pleased with her."

Gone now were the trifles of colored stripes, visible panties, the issues of pay for play and professional teaching. Tennis still had its innate glories, but it was simply unadulterated business and big-time entertainment, and it would not be turned back. The god Money was at the wheel, Tilden might have written. And Hazel had changed. "In her later years," Bud Collins said, "she mellowed quite a bit."

Chapter 12

HAZEL'S DESCENDANTS

IN A RENOVATED TWO-STORY BOSTON VICTORIAN OCCUPIED BY FIVE BACHELORS, the phone rang persistently with the inquiries of young ladies. In 1991, it seemed an odd place to find a shrine to Hazel Hotchkiss Wightman. But even little gray-haired ladies in tennis shoes have fair-haired fans who will not be denied. On one low table in the corner of Robbie Pierce's bedroom is a unique display. It consists of a spread of newspaper and magazine articles, event programs, and pictures fanned out just so, and a commemorative folder from the U.S. Postal Service with Robert Hotchkiss Pierce—Robbie's full name—embossed in gold on it. The folder has a sheet of Olympic stamps inside.

Pierce's mother is the former Wendy Wightman, the daughter of Hazel's son George. And to Robbie, a nice-looking, voluble, dark-haired man of twenty-nine, that makes "Great Grammie" out of Hazel.

Like thousands of people, Robbie remembers the first ritual garage bangboard sessions that his year-younger sister and he were treated to during visits to his great-grandmother's house. They hefted up the sawed-off rackets, played games of consistency to ten, and got candy for rewards. "Get your racket back!" he says was her most memorable refrain.

He remembers in some detail that, as a child, he attended a party in the Boston mayor's office on the fiftieth anniversary of the Wightman Cup, and stunning Chris Evert and Virginia Wade were there. He remembers Great

Gram's invitation to catch a tossed Ping-Pong ball bouncing crazily down the basement steps as part of her everlasting campaign to enhance hand-eye coordination. And who could forget the packages she sent every year!

"We would get these huge boxes of chocolate chip cookies and brownies and lots of dried fruit," he says. "And a lot of second-hand stuff—not stuff she bought.

"And I guess it was a tradition of the Wightman family to give girls a ring on their twenty-first birthday. She had sent one to my mother on her twenty-first, she said, and it was wrapped in old underwear." Pierce smiles at the thought. "But I'd be so excited to see that box when it arrived."

Dutifully, Pierce learned his tennis, not well enough to be a big-ime champion, but well enough to have a few well-deserved seconds in the local spotlight. He rose to be captain of his high school tennis team, for example. And in his junior year, seeded eighth in the city league tournament, he won the thing and got "Athlete of the Week" kudos bestowed by the local newspaper, in Cazanovia, New York. When the newspaper learned of his Hotchkiss connection, it sent out a reporter to interview him. It makes Robbie sad that Great Grammie wasn't alive to see that day. He was proud, and proud of her.

As a child he knew nothing of her fame, of course. He would get kidded about his middle name by other children because it sounded funny. But he didn't get angry. He figured it was some sort of tradition, and he didn't really mind keeping that name going. "It has definitely enriched my life," he says.

Robbie idolizes Hazel's accomplishments as a player, teacher, and organizer, and he deeply admires her total contribution to the game in its historic context. He wishes she were still around to share with him the mysterious source of her boundless energy and her ability to get things done. With her organizational qualities he thinks he could have launched a sports-related career himself. He has attempted to organize certain sports events now as a hobby and thinks it could blossom into a career, if he only had her as a mentor.

Traveling as a college student in London in 1981, though, his avidity almost got him in hot water. He dropped in on Wimbledon during tournament time and suddenly, right there at the International Hall of Fame booth, he discovered an entire section devoted to the Wightman Cup and Great Grammie. He whipped out his camera from his knapsack and started taking a flurry of pictures before anyone could stop him. It was strictly against the rules. When he explained who he was they called the president of the All-England Club to the booth. The gentleman promptly gave Robbie carte blanche to take all the pictures he wanted.

"If you really get to know me," Robbie says, "these stories about Great Grammie eventually come out. I'm just sorry she's not still around. She could introduce me to all sorts of people. People I run into of the older generation always know someone who was taught by her."

The effect of Hazel's involvement in tennis has been long and everlasting to both the Hotchkiss and Wightman sides of a large family (thirteen grandchildren) that's scattered across America like wind-driven pollen. They are a proud clan, smart and resilient. Some are tennis players, others aren't. And whether she was Aunt Hazel or Grammie to them, they accept a special heritage of fame from the western girl who went east and excelled on many levels. The object was to live life to the fullest. Its wrapping paper was tennis. And even if you missed being a championship player, you couldn't miss the message. It whispered through all the trappings and icons of the sport.

As the eldest of her three daughters, Virginia (Henckel), says, "Even our studio portraits of Mother and [her] children show rackets in our hands!"

Naturally, not all the children had Hazel's love or drive for the sport. But everyone learned to play, just as everyone learned to play the piano. Virginia much preferred swimming to tennis, and Hazel (Harlow), the second daughter, confesses, "I was a dud—the worst of the five. I majored in music and was a pianist. I taught for a while. Now I sing. The piano is too lonely.

"Ginny could have been good but she was into swimming. Dotty was the champion."

Dorothy (Hood) says her mother was quite pleased when she won a national junior indoor title, but that was pretty much the height of her acclaim. "I was a tennis groupie," she says, "not a champion. Good in the East, but that was it. I just loved the scene. I played in the nationals in Philadelphia and played in New York, but I had friends there, too, and I looked forward to staying with them."

After Dorothy graduated from Smith in 1944 she stopped playing for thirty years and raised a family. Since her mother's death, she has represented her mother at various commemorations and has been the family spokesperson and authority on her mother's life.

About the only thing daughter Hazel got from tennis, Dorothy says with a laugh, was "good press." One of the Philadelphia papers, dredging up a picture it had of the mother and daughter at the junior nationals one year, ran a picture of the wrong Hazel with the Hazel Wightman obituary in 1974.

No one held as tightly on to the game as Hazel Wightman. She never let go and sowed the seeds until she died.

Lucy Hopman tells the story of how Hazel would hold a cane in one hand and plant it against a garage wall to anchor herself while she taught, holding a racket in the other hand and hitting a ball against the far wall. Lucy is the widow of Harry Hopman, the legendary, hard-driving Aussie Davis Cup coach who retired and settled in America in 1970, then taught at Port Washington Tennis Academy on Long Island. Lucy is also the daughter of George Wightman's sister. That made Hazel her aunt.

"Harry had the same approach to tennis Hazel did," Lucy says. "So one day, must have been around 1972, she called and said come over, she had two talented kids she wanted him to see. He couldn't refuse her, he had so much regard for her.

"They were nice kids I remember, a black boy and girl, twelve and fourteen. I don't remember their names. But I remember her using that stick to steady herself against the wall while she hit the ball with the other. It showed just how indefatigable she was."

As for sportsmanship, she taught by example. Sportsmanship was disciplined behavior, doing the right thing and being polite. In a nutshell, it was simply following the Golden Rule. Competing, she was stiff upper lip all the way, a smile at the end, charitable comments afterward. She didn't like to see anyone lose her temper on the court, whether it was Alice Marble or Billie Jean King. It lacked dignity, she said.

"There's no doubt she was the outstanding woman of the period," Lucy says. "But she wasn't a liberator. She continued playing longer than just about anyone. And she was friendly with the men who ran things—George was USTA president in 1924. But she was very matter-of-fact. I know of no other lady who could accomplish what she did then. She was not an equal. But at least they listened to her."

Her way of being was the old-fashioned American way, simple, plain, and truthful, and she became to tennis what Eleanor Roosevelt was to the nation.

She got letters like the one that began, "Thanks for straightening out my daughter. . . ." Because she emphasized work and ethics in tennis, and her own children were well behaved, she was seen by hundreds of parents in the East as a moral force. If there was a downside in the equation it was that her commitments made her like a working mother of today. Her volunteer hours on the court and with the Red Cross, and her bridge hobby, meant hours away from her own children, who were, to a degree, raised by a nanny.

"There was a period when we had three maids," Hazel, the daughter, says. "But I never felt she neglected us. And as our age was suitable, she then included us in things, like going to California every other year. We all loved that."

Naturally, Hazel's compulsions to keep busy have accrued as a sort of family volume of humor. The stories are legion about how she fought idleness, knitting while playing bridge, writing her book while waiting in her tomato-red car to pick up her children at school, writing newsy postcards to connections all over the world at stoplights and in gas stations while the car tank was filled. Things she didn't want she recycled. It was the ongoing duty of the thrift ethic.

Jim Hotchkiss of Orinda recalls that his aunt's biennial trips to the San Francisco Bay Area were fraught with peculiarities. His father Miller was one of her brothers and had been best man at her Berkeley wedding in 1912.

"After Grandmother died, Aunt Hazel didn't come as regularly," Jim says. "Then she stayed with my father or Marius (another brother). It was sort of with dread that they anticipated her coming, too. Marius was scared to death of her. She'd do things like clean out my father's entire attic, unannounced. When she visited Dotty, Dotty would find all her books rearranged in descending order of height."

Indeed, her visits to her children often resembled inspection tours. Her "suggestions" had a discomfiting edge. Like a good scout, the first one would often call the next in line with advance warning. Still, says daughter Hazel, "she was generous-hearted, a wonderful person whose best trait I think was her sincerity—along with her devotion to duty. I'm just glad she's not alive today, because the world is full of phoniness."

When the women who were closest to her describe her, "strong" is a word they invariably use. The women of the extended family especially felt the heat, that subtle mental shoving that emanated from Grammie. Jane Leonard, Hazel's granddaughter born in 1940 (the oldest daughter of Hazel's oldest daughter, Virginia), says she believes Hazel had a strong effect on women in the tennis community, but relatives were often part of a family display, Hazel's collective image. "It was hard to be related to her because you felt a pressure to be perfect, or at least good," said Jane, who lives in San Francisco but grew up in the East. "She was a celebrity and a mother at the same time. She was a model. I had an image of her, a feeling about her, as a strong woman. And she wanted everyone to reflect well."

As a girl, Jane loved visiting the big house with pictures and memorabilia everywhere, neat hiding places, and lots of kids around so it had the feeling of one big family. "It was a formal kind of house. Everyone was on their best behavior when they went there. It had a maid. It was a kind of house and setting I might read about. It had a romantic image and an aura. But it was homey, too."

She saw Billie Jean King there, and Althea Gibson. Elaborate fluted national trophies were used as water pitchers and vases for dried flowers. She traveled to some tennis camps with her grandmother, and watching her create an imprint she calls up like an old movie. "It seemed she never moved and the balls just kept coming back to her and she kept hitting them back to the kids. She was well into her sixties then."

To her, Grammie was a dynamo. Ping-Pong every night after dinner. At bridge, she was an aggressive, cutthroat player who took risks overbidding but was good at it and knew it. When Jane did well playing, Grammie told her. "It meant a lot because she wasn't liberal with the compliments. You knew you had earned it.

"Grammie did things that most women don't do plus the things they did do. A formidable woman, a doer. She accomplished a lot, and on two levels. She did it in the East at two levels. Boston was and is a class society. And she did what wealthy women did. And then she worked at the grass roots, too.

"But I had no idea of her stature really until she was inducted into the California Women's Sports Hall of Fame in the mid-1970s. They had a brochure and I read all about her titles. She would leave tickets for us for Forest Hills, fancy seats. I began to get an idea of her as a celebrity then. And then the stamp was issued. I have a poster of that now."

In-laws could feel intimidated by her. Yet despite her judgments, she could back off, reassess, and moderate her positions. Although she was opposed to liquor and tobacco, she tolerated them easily at family parties.

"I loved her and she loved me," said daughter-in-law Sally Wightman in an interview. "I got along with her extremely well. She overlooked my faults. She was a remarkable woman."

Sally was sitting in a spacious alcove of the Phillips House Wing at Massachusetts General Hospital and spoke haltingly. The trim and pert Boston lady was bereft and red-eyed yet was able to reminisce. Upstairs, her husband Bill, known in the family affectionately as the fair-haired boy, was going deeper into a coma after a cancer operation which had been followed by a stroke. She gathered herself to pay tribute to her mother-in-law.

"I never heard her give a bad speech," she continued in the empty quiet of the room. "She never bored anyone. Everyone wanted to see her. She would say tennis broadens you—— still playing [at sixty-nine]. They were wonderful speeches. Not intellectual but from the heart. Impromptu, and nice, but heartfelt about the fun and good of tennis, and how you meet people no matter where you go."

Sally paused, then continued. "She had a terrific will to win. I don't think she ever got cross with Bill or me. We saw her almost every Sunday with the children. She'd drive down. Even snowstorms didn't stop her. I think she liked the challenge. She often drove with the brake on."

She smiled and dabbed her eyes. "We played tennis together. She wasn't a bit afraid of telling people what to do on the court. I'd make the errors.

"She loved to eat. She helped with the cooking but she wasn't a cook. She liked doing the cookies. She was infallible in that. She loved cats. They had the run of the house." One of the cats was named Oski, after the Cal yell that cheered her on at the 1924 Olympics.

The two women had similar childhoods, and that allowed Sally to ask the older woman questions that perhaps she mightn't have been asked otherwise.

"I learned a lot driving her home on Sundays. I was a tomboy. She had four brothers. She liked telling about those times. I was a little scared of her before I was married, though. I still meet people who say they were scared of her. I wanted to go out and have a cigarette—well, she was right about that, all right.

"She went to some Red Sox games with her father-in-law. They got along very well. She said he told her, 'Stick with me and you'll wear diamonds,' and she did."

Hazel was generous with her finances with everyone, Sally said. But she was no spendthrift, until it came to tennis tickets.

"They couldn't give her a ticket anywhere. At the nationals at Longwood she would buy them by the fistful. She'd call and say, 'I've got all these tickets, can you use some?' Well, of course I could. I loved that!"

Chapter 13

HONORS

TENNIS IS LIKE WATER AND PEOPLE ARE LIKE PEBBLES DROPPING INTO IT, making their impact, creating concentric circles. Out on the edge, where the largest circle is, is the legacy of Hazel Hotchkiss Wightman. She has been described as the mother of women's tennis, the grand dame of tennis, the First Lady, the grassroots teacher of all time, the innovator, the pioneer.

Almost forgotten now is the fact she practically invented the volley for women. And while winning more than one hundred forty tournaments in a lifetime doesn't begin to push the current record books, it is doubtful someone at age sixty-seven will win a national 40's doubles tournament, as she did in 1954. And it will be an astronomical long shot if anyone equals her rankings as a mother. After her main tennis career, she stopped to get married and raise a family, then resumed as time would allow. In 1915 and 1918 she was the number two ranking woman in the nation, and in 1919, as the mother of three, she was number one. But these are merely records.

Her contribution is still being felt and will be for at least the life of the generations she touched. Thousands on the East Coast knew her largesse. She was, as Nancy Norton described her, "the ministering angel of tangle-footed tennis players. . . ."

Here, from the book *One Hundred Years of Longwood* by Robert Minton, is how she typically spent her days at age seventy-three. This is from a letter she wrote to *New York Times* sports writer Allison Danzig:

"I had only eight girls staying at my house during the week of the National Doubles, which was quite a change and very simple.... Two and three times a week youngsters come to my garage for instruction and sometimes eight or ten are there at a time.... I still captain the team on Monday mornings at the Red Cross canteen and the Friday morning Medical Center Lunch Shop Team. Two other mornings I do a few hours a week of Red Cross sewing, and once a week I have an enjoyable ladies' doubles at tennis, where two of the players are considerably younger than my other friend and me. Now and then I get a few thirteen-year-olds on the court to run them around. I get a couple of bridge games in each week, too."

In her later years Hazel was honored many, many times. She received hundreds of cards and letters every year that testified to her considerable following. People whom she had touched were continually remembering their personal experiences. Here is one from Southern California's Pat Henry Yeomans, in a letter dated August 22, 1973, the fiftieth anniversary of the Wightman Cup:

> Dear Hazel,
>
> The August issue of *Tennis USA*, with your picture on the front and story by Ed Baker, made my cup runneth over with wonderful memories.
>
> All those years with all your tennis players running in and out of the house—Kay Hubbell and Nancy Norton cooking pies and turkeys—changing the sheets on the beds in your home and across the street for our Junior Wightman Cup girls—assisting all the visiting Californians....
>
> I'll bet there were times when you thought there was no end to Californians arriving on your doorstep with tennis racquets—and requests for hospitality.
>
> This year I know you are delighted that 'one of your girls'—Edy Anne McGoldrick—will receive the Service Bowl. She deserves it—she has made the transition for women's tennis [to pro tennis] in a dignified way. It always takes work, planning, effort, and imagination.

But that's living life to the hilt.
You showed us how!
May your joys increase and this be the happiest year for you and your family—and best wishes to all who have been blessed to be touched by your love and friendship.
As I have.

Nancy Norton, mentioned in that letter, was one of those not particularly athletically gifted girls who nevertheless learned the game through Hazel's free group lessons and loved playing and watching. She was so grateful, and so moved by the generosity of the older woman, that she became devoted to Hazel, volunteering her domestic assistance for several summers when she was in college. Norton went on to become a college history professor, a book author, and a major tennis volunteer whose appreciable committee work, plus rankings in senior competition, earned her a spot in the New England Lawn Tennis Hall of Fame.

She felt she saw where the real test of Mrs. Wightie was.

"We 'ordinary' were the challenge and meaning of her life," Norton observed in the program commemorating the fiftieth year of the Wightman Cup. "Sometimes the criticism [from her] seems harsh, unrealistic. For if Mrs. Wightman gives, she also demands—the best in you. It is a measure of her caring. It is the best in you that makes life satisfactory."

Kay Hubbell was a better player, competing at a higher level, but she felt the same about giving back to Hazel and contributing to the scene that supported the historic parade of stars through the famous house.

Pat Henry Yeomans is a lifelong tournament player and former girls' national 18's champion (1935). She's also an amateur historian whose areas of expertise are women's tennis before the Open era, Southern California tennis, and especially the eminent Los Angeles Tennis Club which her father, the late Bill Henry, sports editor of the *Los Angeles Times*, helped found.

More than anyone in the ranks of senior women players, Yeomans has kept an awareness of past champions and heroes alive by personally promoting them among players. Significantly, in 1956 she won something called the Service Bowl Award from the United States Tennis Association. The 1950 winner of that same award was Nancy Norton, and the winner in 1958 was Kay Hubbell.

This award by the five-hundred-thousand-member organization is traditionally given to the woman player who ". . . yearly makes the most notable contribution to the Sportsmanship, Fellowship, and Service of Tennis."

The award has an unusual history. Originally, an association of about thirty New England women would get together for an annual tennis party hosted by Mrs. Lyman H. B. Olmstead. One year they decided an award ought to be given to the woman in the New England Lawn Tennis Association best fitting the above description. Hazel Wightman was the first recipient in 1940. Four years later, the bowl, donated by Mrs. Olmstead, became a national award under the aegis of the USTA, which specifies today, when it is awarded at a ceremony at the U.S. Open championships, that it is "to honor the example of Mrs. Hazel H. Wightman."

Hazel won it again in 1946 and has probably directly influenced more than three-fourths of the recipients, including Billie Jean King and Chris Evert. Winning the bowl in 1973 was Edy Anne McGoldrick, then serving her second year as captain of the Wightman Cup team. A program note from that time observed that the mother of six was "making her mark as the first significant female administrator in the male-dominated U.S. Lawn Tennis Association." But it was first as a girl that she met Hazel Wightman, when McGoldrick's mother, Mrs. John Sullivan of Belmont, had turned her and her brothers over to Hazel to instruct them in the ways of tennis. In an interview in 1991 Mrs. Sullivan compared Hazel Wightman and her accomplishments to Eleanor Roosevelt. Mrs. Sullivan was one of hundreds of parents who took their children to Hazel, expecting that through tennis their offspring would learn early on some of the many complex lessons of life. Tennis was a vehicle to self-improvement and self-realization.

The East has been so affected by the Hazel Wightman example there is even a sizable tennis club named after her. The Wightman family has no financial connection to it at all. It is just a tennis club built in 1970 in Weston, Massachusetts, which wanted a set of sterling standards to guide its membership forever. Mrs. Wightman stood for the right stuff. Gladly the family approved the club's use of her name, and she attended the Hazel Hotchkiss Wightman Tennis Center opening in 1970. In her eighties then, she even gave a talk and some lessons.

"Dedicating the Center to Mrs. Wightman wasn't just a whim of the Board of Governors," it is written in the club's history. "To our membership she is our inspiration. It is to her ideals that the Wightman Tennis Center is dedicated."

Hazel Wightman obviously enjoyed this sort of reaffirming attention. Never, though, would she make a fuss over awards and acclaim, or take them for granted. Oohing and ahhing over President Nixon's congratulatory telegram on her eighty-sixth birthday would have been out of character, for example. Saving it would not.

It was not just the universal truths Hazel propounded that attracted organizations like the tennis club, it was the image and character of Hazel herself. She insisted on calling women's draws "ladies'" draws in the countless tournaments she ran at Longwood and other venues in the East. It was a matter of image, appropriate to the time. At the same time she was plain-talking, level-headed, and heavy on the control-is-within-your-grasp attitude. This from a woman of high social station where haughtiness is part of the stereotype. As her granddaughter Hazel "Baysie" Wightman, daughter of Sally and William, says, "She was a big deal, a Boston social lady. She had her bridge-playing buddies who had Monets on the wall. But she was more of the earth. Not a snob. She was a merit person, and not into [social register] connections."

A large oil painting of her hangs over a fireplace mantel on the main floor of the Wightman Tennis Center, where bridge is the dominant game, played presumably with the same verve for winning she had. "She wasn't above bragging a bit about beating the men at billiards, either," Baysie Wightman says with a wink.

The year 1973 was the crest of Hazel's international involvement. The Wightman Cup was still quite healthy and enjoying its silver anniversary at the Longwood Cricket Club. On Friday, August 24, the day of the first matches, when many former players and captains were present and the first round of parties was over, this press notice was released from Boston's British Consulate:

"It has been announced from Buckingham Palace on the occasion of the fiftieth Anniversary of the Wightman Cup matches that Her Majesty Queen Elizabeth II has conferred an honour on Mrs. Hazel Hotchkiss Wightman, the donor of the Wightman Cup, in recognition of her services to international tennis and her contribution to Anglo-American friendship.

"Mrs. Wightman has been appointed an honorary Commander of the

Order of the British Empire (O.B.E.)."

The honor, originated in 1917 by King George V, is made to civilians for distinguished public service.

Hazel had been inducted into the International Tennis Hall of Fame in 1957, the same year as R. N. "Dick" Williams, her injured Olympic mixed doubles partner. On behalf of the citizenry, she had been awarded the Boston Medal of Achievement in 1967 for the distinction she had brought to the city. Before and after these she acquired a raft of citations and commendations from various groups, including enshrinement in four more halls of fame: Northern California Tennis Hall of Fame, New England Lawn Tennis Association, the University of California at Berkeley's Women's Athletic Hall, where she was the first, and the Intercollegiate Women's Hall of Fame. But the O.B.E. was the single greatest honor because recognizing Mrs. Wightman in this way implied that tennis was a sublime vehicle for bringing nations together: tennis in her hands was arms across the sea. And for all of her "unassuming modesty," as her citation from Brookline's Brotherhood Temple Beth Zion once described her, she wore the O.B.E. medal to every formal affair thereafter like a little general.

What came posthumously, and as a total surprise to her family, was the Olympic postage stamp in 1990 with her likeness on it. What qualified her as a candidate for the Olympic series of five unique medal-winning Olympians, including the famous speedster Jesse Owens from the 1936 Berlin games, was that she had won two gold medals in tennis in 1924, and she was deceased.

She was the only tennis player ever to show up on a U.S. Postage stamp. Oddly, the likeness on the stamp, an action shot, really more resembled Helen Wills's form in hitting a running forehand than Hazel's. Ideally, the shot should have been a volley, Hazel's signature, symbolizing an evolutionary shift that gave rise to serve-and-volley stylists such as Alice Marble, Althea Gibson, and Martina Navratilova. That's the style Hazel would have adopted, too, if she had been taller and the serving rules hadn't prohibited crossing the baseline until the served ball landed. As it was, she was only tall enough to stand as a beacon in women's tennis for the better part of a century.

It was a simple game she began at the urging of her brothers, merely to improve her health.

APPENDIX A

Records of American Wightman Cup Players and Leading British Players
from the official USTA Yearbook

American Wightman Cup Players

Hazel Hotchkiss Wightman, donor of the cup, played in and won the longest doubles match, forty games, alongside Eleanor Goss of the U.S., when they defeated Mrs. Phyllis Covell and Kathleen McKane 10-8, 5-7, 6-4 in the series opener of 1923.

Jane Albert, 1966, 0-1 in doubles.
Penelope Anderson, 1928, 0-1 in doubles.
Dorothy Andrus, 1935, 0-1 in doubles.
Julie Anthony, 1975, 0-1 in doubles.
Ethel B. Arnold, 1935, 1-1 in singles.
Mary Arnold, 1939, 0-1 in doubles.
Miriam Arnold, 1958, 0-1 in singles.
Jeanne Arth, 1959, 1-0 in doubles.
Tracy Austin, 1978, 1979, 1981, 4-2 in singles, 2-0 in doubles.
    Overall: 6-2 in 3 matches.
Carolin Babcock, 1933, 1934, 1935, 1936, 1-2 in singles, 1-2 in doubles.
    Overall: 2-4 in 4 matches.
Jane Bartkowicz, 1968, 1969, 1970, 2-0 in singles, 2-0 in doubles.
    Overall: 4-0 in 3 matches.
Pauline Betz, 1946, 2-0 in singles, 1-0 in doubles.
    Overall: 3-0 in 1 match.
Justina Bricka, 1961, 1-0 in singles.

Louise Brough, 1946, 1947, 1948, 1950, 1952, 1953, 1954, 1955, 1956, 1957, 12-0 in singles, 10-0 in doubles.
    Overall: 22-0 in 10 matches.
Mary K. Browne, 1925, 1926, 0-2 in singles, 1-1 in doubles.
    Overall: 1-3 in 2 matches.
Dorothy M. Bundy, 1937, 1938, 1939, 1-2 in doubles
May Sutton Bundy, 1925, 0-1 in doubles.
Elise Burgin, 1986, 1-0 in doubles.
Jennifer Capriati, 1989, 1-0 in singles.
Rosemary Casals, 1967, 1976, 1977, 1979, 1980, 1981, 1982, 1-3 in singles, 6-1 in doubles.
    Overall: 7-4 in 7 matches.
Nancy Chaffee, 1951, 1-0 in doubles.
Charlotte H. Chapin, Jr., 1927, 0-1 in doubles.
Maureen Connolly, 1951, 1952, 1953, 1954, 7-0 in singles, 2-0 in doubles.
    Overall: 9-0 in 4 matches.
Edith Cross, 1929, 1930, 1-0 in singles, 0-2 in doubles.
    Overall: 1-2 in 2 matches
Josephine Cruickshank, 1934, 0-1 in doubles.
Mary Ann Eisel Curtis, 1966, 1967, 1968, 1969, 1970, 1971, 1-2 in singles, 3-3 in doubles.
    Overall: 4-5 in 6 matches.
Stephanie DeFina, 1968, 0-1 in doubles.
Margaret Osborne duPont, 1946, 1947, 1948, 1949, 1950, 1954, 1955, 1957, 1961, 1962, 19-0 in singles, 9-0 in doubles.
    Overall: 19-0 in 10 matches.
Chris Evert, 1971, 1972, 1973, 1975, 1976, 1977, 1978, 1979, 1980, 1981, 1982, 1984, 1985, 26-0 in singles, 8-4 in doubles.
    Overall: 34-4 in 13 matches.
Jeanne Evert, 1973, 1974, 0-1 in singles. 1-0 in doubles.
    Overall: 1-1 in 2 matches.
Sarah Palfrey Fabyan, 1930, 1931, 1932, 1933, 1934, 1935, 1936, 1937, 1938, 1939, 7-4 in singles, 7-3 in doubles.
    Overall: 14-7 in 10 matches.
Karol Fageros, 1958, 0-1 in doubles.

Donna F. Fales, 1963, 1964, 1-1 in doubles.
Patty Fendick, 1988, 1989, 1-0 in singles, 1-0 in doubles.
   Overall: 2-0 in 2 matches.
Gigi Fernandez, 1987, 1988, 2-0 in doubles.
   Overall: 2-0 in matches.
Mary Joe Fernandez, 1989, 2-0 in singles, 1-0 in doubles.
   Overall: 3-0 in 1 match.
Beverly Baker Fleitz, 1949, 1956, 1959 3-0 in singles, 1-0 in doubles.
   Overall: 4-0 in 3 matches.
Shirley Fry. 1949-51, 1952, 1953, 1955, 1956, 4-2 in singles, 6-0 in doubles.
   Overall: 10-2 in 6 matches.
Bonnie Gadusek, 1986, 2-0 in singles, 1-0 in doubles.
   Overall: 3-0.
Zina Garrison, 1987, 1988, 3-1 in singles, 1-1 in doubles.
   Overall: 4-2 in 2 matches.
Althea Gibson, 1957, 1958, 3-1 in singles, 2-0 in doubles.
   Overall: 5-1 in 2 matches.
Eleanor Goss, 1923, 1924, 1925, 1926, 1927, 1928, 1-2 in singles, 2-3 in doubles.
   Overall: 3-5 in 6 matches.
Carole Caldwell Graebner, 1963, 1964, 1965, 1967, 1971, 2-0 in singles, 2-2 in doubles.
   Overall: 4-2 in 4 matches.
Mona Schallau Guerrant, 1974, 1975, 1976, 0-2 in singles, 2-1 in doubles.
   Overall: 2-3 in 3 matches.
Darlene Hard, 1957, 1959, 1960, 1962, 1963, 6-3 in singles. 4-1 in doubles.
   Overall: 10-4 in 5 matches.
Anna M. Harper, 1931, 1932, 1-1 in singles, 1-1 in doubles.
   Overall: 2-2 in 22 matches.
Doris Hart, 1946, 1947, 1948, 1949, 1950, 1951, 1952, 1953, 1954, 1955, 14-0 in singles, 8-1 in doubles.
   Overall: 22-1 in 10 matches.
Kathy Harter, 1968, 0-1 in doubles.
Julie M. Heldman, 1969, 1970, 1971, 1974, 3-3 in singles, 2-1 in doubles.
   Overall: 5-4 in 4 matches.

Patti Hogan, 1972, 1973, 2-1 in singles, 2-0 in doubles.
   Overall: 4-1 in 2 matches.
Terry Holladay, 1976 1-0 in singles.
Janet Hopps, 1958, 1959, 1960, 0-1 in singles, 1-2 in doubles.
   Overall: 1-3 in 3 matches.
Helen Jacobs, 1927, 1928, 1929, 1930, 1931, 1932, 1933, 1934, 1935, 1936, 1937, 1939, 14-7 in singles, 5-4 in doubles.
   Overall: 19-11 in 12 matches.
Andrea Jaeger, 1980, 1981, 2-1 in singles, 1-0 in doubles.
   Overall: 3-1 in 2 matches.
Marion Z. Jessup, 1924, 1926, 1-0 in singles, 1 -1 in doubles.
   Overall: 2-1 in 2 matches.
Kathy Jordan, 1979, 1980, 1-1 in singles, 1-0 in doubles.
   Overall: 2-1 in 2 matches.
Billie Jean Moffitt King, 1961, 1962, 1963, 1964, 1965, 1966, 1967, 1970, 1977, 1978, 14-2 in singles, 7-3 in doubles.
   Overall: 21-5 in 10 matches
Ann Kiyomura, 1976, 1979, 2-0 in doubles.
Dorothy H. Knode, 1955, 1956, 1957, 1958, 1960, 4-2 in singles, 1-2 in doubles.
   Overall: 5-4 in 5 matches.
Molla Bjurstedt Mallory, 1923, 1924, 1925, 1927, 1928 5-5 in singles, 1-1 in doubles.
   Overall: 6-6 in 5 matches,
Alice Marble, 1933, 1937, 1938, 1939, 5-1 in singles, 3-1 in doubles.
   Overall: 6-2 in 4 matches.
Lori McNeil, 1987-88-89, 5-0 in singles, 2-1 in doubles.
   Overall: 7-1 in 3 matches.
Helen Wills Moody, 1923, 1924, 1925, 1927, 1928, 1929, 1930, 1931, 1932, 1938, 18-2 in singles, 3-7 in doubles.
   Overall: 21-9 in 1-0 matches.
Sally Moore, 1959, 0-1 in singles, 0-1 in doubles.
   Overall: 0-2 in 1 match.
Gertrude Moran, 1949, 1-0 in doubles.
Alycia Moulton, 1984, 0-1 in singles, 1-0 in doubles.

Overall: 1-1 in 1 match.

Betsy Nagelsen, 1974, 1985, 1988, 1989, 3-1 in doubles.
Overall: 3-1 in 4 matches.

Martina Navratilova, 1983, 2-0 in singles, 1-0 in doubles.
Overall: 3-0 in 1 match.

Janet Newberry, 1974, 1975, 0-3 in singles, 0-2 in doubles.
Overall: 0-5 in 2 matches.

Wendy Overton, 1972, 0-2 in singles, 1-0 in doubles.
Overall: 1-2 in 1 match.

Kristy Pigeon, 1971, 0-1 in singles.

Barbara Potter, 1982, 1984, 3-1 in singles, 2-0 in doubles.
Overall: 5-1 in 2 matches.

Marita Redondo, 1973, 0-1 in doubles.

Stephanie Rehe, 1986, 1-0 in singles.

Candy Reynolds, 1983, 0-1 in doubles.

Nancy Richey, 1962, 1963, 1964, 1965, 1966, 1967, 1968, 1969, 1970, 9-7 in singles, 3-2 in doubles.
Overall: 12-9 in 9 matches.

Kathy Rinaldi, 1983, 1985, 1986, 4-0 in singles. 1-0 in doubles.
Overall: 5-0 in 3 matches.

JoAnne Russell, 1977, 1-0 in doubles.

Elizabeth Ryan, 1926, 1-1 in singles, 1-0 in doubles.
Overall: 2-1 in 1 match.

Pam Shriver, 1978, 1981, 1983, 1985, 1987, 6-1 in singles, 3-1 in doubles.
Overall: 9-2 in 5 matches.

Anne Smith, 1980, 1982, 1-0 in singles, 1-1 in doubles.
Overall: 2-1 in 2 matches.

Paula Smith, 1983, 0-1 in doubles.

Karen Hantze Susman, 1960, 1961, 1962, 1965, 3-3 in singles, 3-0 in doubles.
Overall: 6-3 in 4 matches.

Patricia C. Todd, 1947, 1948, 1949, 1950, 1951, 4-1 in doubles.

Linda Tuero, 1973, 1-0 in singles.

Marjorie G. Van Ryn, 1933, 1936, 1937, 1-2 in doubles.

Margaret Varner, 1961, 1962, 2-0 in doubles.

Sharon Walsh, 1982, 1984, 2-0 in doubles.

Anne White, 1985, 1986, 2-0 in doubles.
Robin White, 1987, 1-0 in doubles.
Hazel H. Wightman, 1923, 1924, 1927, 1929, 1931, 3-2 in doubles.
Valerie Ziegenfuss, 1969, 1971, 1972, 1-0 in singles, 2-1 in doubles.
   Overall: 3-1 in 3 matches.

Leading British Players

Sue Barker, 1974, 1975, 1976, 1977, 1978, 1979, 1980, 1981, 1982, 5-13 in singles, 4-4 in doubles.
   Overall: 9-17 in 9 matches.
Kathleen McKane Godfree, 1923, 1924, 1925, 1926, 1927, 1930, 1934, 5-5 in singles, 2-5 in doubles.
   Overall:11-16 in 7 matches.
Christine Truman Janes, 1957, 1958, 1959, 1960, 1961, 1962, 1963, 1967, 1968, 1969, 1971, 6-12 in singles, 5-4 in doubles.
   Overall: 10-15 in 11 matches.
Ann Haydon Jones, 1957, 1958, 1959, 1960, 1961, 1962-, 1963, 1964, 1965, 1966, 1967, 1970, 1975, 10-11 in singles, 6-5 in doubles.
   Overall: 16-16 in 13 matches.
Kay Stammers Menzies, 1935, 1936, 1937, 1938, 1939, 1946, 1947, 1948, 4-9 in singles, 1-4 in doubles.
   Overall: 5-13 in 8 matches.
Angela Mortimer, 1953, 1955, 1956, 1959, 1960, 1961, 3-7 in singles, 1-4 in doubles.
   Overall: 4-11 in 6 matches.
Betty Nuthall, 1927, 1928, 1929, 1931, 1932, 1933, 1934, 1939, 3-5 in singles, 3-2 in doubles.
   Overall: 62-7 in 8 matches.
Virginia Wade, 1965, 1966, 1967, 1968, 1969, 1970, 1971, 1972, 1973, 1974, 1975, 1976, 1977, 1978, 1979, 1980, 1981, 1982, 1983, 1984, 19-85, 12-23 in singles, 7-13 in doubles.
   Overall: 19-36 in 21 matches.
Phoebe Holcroft Watson, 1928, 1929, 1930, 3-3 in singles, 3-0 in doubles.
   Overall: 6-3 in 3 matches.

APPENDIX B

Major Titles

Hazel Hotchkiss Wightman

United States National Women's Singles 1909, 1910, 1911, 1919

United States National Women's Doubles
    1909 with Miss Edith E. Rotch
    1910 with Miss Edith E. Rotch
    1911 with Miss Eleonora Sears
    1915 with Miss Eleonora Sears
    1924 with Miss Helen N. Wills

United States National Mixed Doubles
    1909 with Wallace F. Johnson
    1910 with Joseph R. Carpenter, Jr.
    1911 with Wallace F. Johnson
    1915 with Harry C. Johnson
    1918 with Irving C. Wright
    1920 with Wallace F. Johnson

United States National Indoor Women's Singles 1919, 1927

United States National Indoor Women's Doubles
    1919 with Marion Zinderstein
    1921 with Marion Zinderstein
    1924 with Marion Z. Jessup
    1927 with Marion Z. Jessup

1928 with Sarah Palfrey
1929 with Sarah Palfrey
1930 with Sarah Palfrey
1931 with Sarah Palfrey
1933 with Sarah Palfrey
1943 with Pauline Betz

United States National Indoor Mixed Doubles
1923 with Burnham N. Dell
1924 with William T. Tilden, 2nd
1926 with G. P. Gardner, Jr.
1927 with G. P. Gardner, Jr.
1928 with Henry L. Johnson, Jr.

United States National Clay Court Mixed Doubles
1915 with Harry C. Johnson

United States National Grass Court Women's Forty Doubles
1940 with Edith Sigourney
1941 with Edith Sigourney
1942 with Molly T. Fremont-Smith
1944 with Edith Sigourney
1946 with Edith Sigourney
1947 with Edith Sigourney
1948 with Marion Z. Jessup
1949 with Marjorie G. Buck
1950 with Marjorie G. Buck
1952 with Marjorie G. Buck
1954 with Nell Hopman

International Titles
Wimbledon Women's Doubles 1924 with Helen Wills
Olympic gold medal Women's Doubles 1924 with Helen Wills
Olympic gold medal Mixed Doubles 1924 with R. Norris (Dick) Williams

APPENDIX C

Sources

Books

Barrett, John, editor. *World of Tennis 1974*. Compiled by Lance Tingay. New York: Popular Library, 1974.

Barrett, John, editor. *World of Tennis 1975*. Compiled by Lance Tingay. New York: Popular Library, 1975.

Clerici, Gianni. *The Ultimate Tennis Book*. Chicago: Follett, 1975.

Cummings, Parke. *American Tennis*. Boston: Little Brown, 1957.

Danzig, Allison, editor. *The Fireside Book of Tennis*. New York: Simon & Schuster, 1972.

Engelmann, Larry. *The Goddess and the American Girl*. New York: Oxford University Press, 1988.

Hart, Stan. *Once a Champion*. New York: Dodd, Mead & Co., 1985.

Jacobs, Helen Hull. *Beyond the Game*. Philadelphia: J.B. Lippincott, 1936.

Minton, Robert. *Illustrated History of Forest Hills*. J.B. Philadelphia: Lippincott Co., 1975.

_____. *One Hundred Years of Longwood*. Lynn, Massachusetts: H.O. Zimman, 1977.

Schickel, Richard. *The World of Tennis*. Toronto: Random House of Canada Ltd., 1975.

Tilden, Bill. *Match Play and the Spin of the Ball*. Pt. Washington, New York: Kennicat Press, 1960.

Tinling, Ted. *Love and Faults,*. New York: Crown, 1979.

United States Tennis Association Yearbook, 1994 . Lynn, Massachusetts: H.O. Zimman, Inc., 1994.

Wightman, Hazel Hotchkiss. *Better Tennis*. Boston: Houghton Mifflin Co., 1933.

Wills, Helen. *Fifteen-Thirty*. New York: Charles Scribners & Sons, 1937.

Yeomans, Patricia Henry.*Southern California Tennis Champions and Centennial 1887-1987*. Los Angeles: Southern California Committee for the Olympic Games, 1987.

Articles

American Lawn Tennis magazine, various issues, 1907-1911

Kaplan, Janice. "Foremothers."

Klaw, Barbara. "Queen Mother of Tennis: An Interview with Hazel Hotchkiss Wightman." *American Heritage* (August 1975).

Maddocks, Melvin. "The Original Little Old Lady in Tennis Shoes." *Sports Illustrated* (April 10, 1972).

Norton, Nancy. "A History and a Tribute, Hazel Hotchkiss Wightman." *50th Anniversary Wightman Cup Matches*, program (August, 1973).

Wills, Helen. "Unforgettable Mrs. Wightie." *Reader's Digest* (October, 1977).

Wind, Herbert Warren. "Run, Helen!" *The New Yorker* (August 30, 1952).

_____. "The Sporting Scene: From Wimbledon to Forest Hills—A Summer to Remember." *The New Yorker* (October 13, 1975).

Newspapers

Boston Globe
Christian Science Monitor
Healdsburg Herald
Leicester Chronicle
Oakland Tribune
San Francisco Chronicle

Interviews

Dodo Bundy Cheney
Louise Brough Clapp
Bud Collins
Sarah Palfrey Danzig
Bill Drake
Margaret Osborne duPont
Hazel (Wightman) Harlow

Virginia Henckel
Dorothy Hood
Lucy Hopman
James Hotchkiss
Billie Jean King
Jane Leonard
Nancy Norton
Robert Pierce
Edith Sullivan
George H. Wightman
Hazel (Baysie) Wightman
Sally Wightman
Pat Yeomans

APPENDIX D

Museums and Exhibitons

Major Museums
Women's Collegiate Tennis Hall of Fame, College of William and Mary
International Tennis Hall of Fame, Newport, RI

Some Memorabelia
Healdsburg Historical Society, Healdsburg, CA
University of California, Berkeley, CA

BETTER TENNIS

by
Hazel Hotchkiss Wightman

Boston and New York
HOUGHTON MIFFLIN COMPANY
The Riverside Press Cambridge
1933

To
The Young Tennis-Players
Of California
And Massachusetts

FOREWORD

DEAR MRS. WIGHTMAN,

I am so happy to hear that you are writing a book on tennis for girl and women players. You should have done so before this, because you have so much to tell that is both interesting and helpful, not only for the beginner but for the more experienced player who takes part in tournaments. I feel that your advice will be helpful to my game, even though I have been playing in tournaments for more than ten years.

I remember that when we played together there always seemed to be something new to learn. It wasn't as if everything had been mastered and catalogued. You made me see that in tennis, the interesting and amusing situations and possibilities are infinite. It is this very thing that has held your interest in the game and that, in my mind, has established tennis as a pastime of which it is impossible to become weary. At your house in Brookline, I discovered that ice cream and chocolate sauce are good for the forehand drive; and at the Longwood Cricket Club, while playing tennis with you, I learned that it is a good idea to remind oneself to keep one's brain working. In other words, it helps one's game *to think*.

When I am reminded of the way that you play tennis, I realize that the game is a supremely logical one. The frame of mind with which you approach it — call it point of view if you wish — should be described in your book, and I hope that you will give a chapter to it.

I smile to myself in remembering our Wightman Cup doubles match at Wimbledon, when an American women's team went abroad for the first time to play against the English. We had lost all of the singles matches. The English team of Kathleen MacKane and Evelyn Colyer was literally ready to eat us up in the final match of the series. You looked very tiny on the great green expanse of the Center Court, and our opponents probably thought that your opposition would not be very formidable. Mine they didn't count at all, because they had discovered in the singles that I was inexperienced in international competition.

I felt calm and collected, however, in the doubles, and the possibility of defeat seemed remote in my mind. I was full of confidence, inspired by your presence on the court.

Your game was full of wise strategy, surprising angles, and headwork. It seemed as if your balls were too good to be true. Although some balls in a tennis game may be good without being true, a ball that is true is always good. The quality of trueness comes first, and goodness follows. What is true of true tennis balls is often true of the people who play with them. There are true tennis balls and true tennis players, and you are one of the latter!

When the last ball in the Wightman Cup doubles was put away that day on the Center Court, I am sure that our opponents were aware of the fact that you were a splendid doubles player.

An English team made another attempt to overcome the captain and her young lieutenant in the finals at the Wimbledon Championships, which were held shortly after. At the Olympic Games in Paris, they tried again.

The Olympic encounter was perhaps our most exciting against a British team. We lagged behind in the third set. The wind was blowing across the desolate fields of Colombes, and it seemed as if the dust from the red clay court rose in whirlwinds, especially on our side of the net. But it must have done so on both sides of the net.

I learned in that match the value of the word "scramble." "Yours!" you said when a short ball came over the net on my side of the court at a crucial moment in the match. If it had not been for the command in your voice as you anticipated the drop shot, I would have remained with my feet glued to the court. To slide, lunge, dive, does not conform to good style in tennis, but there is the dignity of sincerity in the scramble.

Boasting cannot be forgiven unless it is of achievement made possible by someone other than oneself —and then credit must be placed where it is due.

So, with pride, I remind you that our career in tournament doubles was never marred by defeat. This was because you knew the game, its angles, how to make the best possible shot for each situation in the play. At the same time, you inspired your partner with confidence and were able, with your understanding of human nature as well as of the game, to make a team a smooth working unit rather than a combination of players, each of whom was playing a game of singles on the doubles court.

No one is better qualified to write a book about tennis than are you, both on the singles and on the doubles game. I look forward to it and shall enjoy seeing in print those tennis truths which I learned during the pleasant years when you were the little general and I the youthful lieutenant.

Yours affectionately,

HELEN WILLS

CONTENTS

My Tennis Story	173
How I Began to Play	174
I Learn to Keep the Ball in Play	174
My First Tournaments	175
National Championships	177
Maurice McLoughlin	177
The Eastern Circuit	178
A Definite Objective	179
Back in the Game	179
Helen Wills	180
Indoor Tournaments	180
Olympic Tennis	181
Great Women Players	182
Sarah Palfrey	183
Suzanne Lenglen	184
Teaching Children	185
Advice for the Beginner	186
Why Some Players Develop Faster	188
Strokes	189
The Forehand	192
The Backhand	193
The Serve and the Smash	193
The Drive	195
The Volley	196

Balance and Rhythm	197
Shoulders	198
Position on the Court	199
Tactics	200
Angles	201
Returns	203
Mental Attitude	204
Don't Defeat Yourself	204
It's an Ill Wind	205
Doubles	206
Information in Doubles	207
Strategy in Doubles	207
Position in Doubles	208
Teamwork	209
A Word to Teachers	211
Appendix	212
Slogans and Maxims	214
A Tennis Alphabet	216

BETTER TENNIS
My Tennis Story

THOUGH MY PURPOSE IN WRITING THIS BOOK IS TO STATE THE FUNDAMENTAL principles of tennis, I suppose some account of my own tennis career will be of interest and will enforce the points I want to make.

Before I begin, I should like to say that tennis has never been my career in the sense of being my sole absorbing interest. My life has been full and happy, with tennis thrown in for good measure. How could a college girl, a young housekeeper, or a mother of five children —I have been all of these during the time of my championship play —give undistracted attention to any sport! I could not, and it is not necessary to do so, in my opinion, to get the greatest pleasure and benefit from the game. My days have been like those of thousands of other American wives and mothers who grapple with the problems of home-making and child-rearing. My children have been my chief preoccupation, their education, their health, their diet, their hair, and their baths my personal responsibility. I emphasize all this because of the encouragement it may afford to people who think they have no time in their lives for any form of sport, and to avoid giving a false impression when I begin to discuss the game. While it has not been the chief interest of my life, tennis, as you will gather from the following pages, has been to me not only a stimulating pastime, but a builder of character and health, and a channel of intensified life, dramatic, rhythmic, and beautiful. To express my gratitude for it and to encourage other players is the object of this book.

Now for my own tennis story. Like any other, it is made up of light and shade, of alternate victories and defeats. I do not know which helped me more. Perhaps when you read the brief history of my tournament play, you will suspect that I have had more than my share of victories and may conclude that my enjoyment and enthusiasm spring from my success. But I think that is not the case. I enjoy the game, win or lose, and I am deeply convinced that that is the only spirit in which to play.

How I Began to Play

I was rather delicate as a child and subject to frequent headaches, so I was not allowed to stay in school very long at a time and was urged to play games as an inducement to stay out of doors. As a result, I developed a great fondness for games, especially for playing ball. I still enjoy playing catch, or throwing a ball against a wall, both of which, by the way, are a good foundation on which to build tennis skill. Another hobby of mine was pole-vaulting, and I might have been seen almost any day vaulting over the various gates and fences on our ranch. As there were few girls in our community, I usually played with my four brothers on their football and baseball teams. Knowing that I should not be wanted on a team of any kind if I were not a help, I worked hard not to be classed as a "sissy," and as a result was usually picked early when sides were being chosen. At other times, I had wonderful sport knocking "sky-balls" for my brothers and their friends to catch in our big field.

When I was about fourteen, however, my family left Healdsburg, California, and went to live in Berkeley. There in the city I was not allowed to play out on the pavements with the boys and soon showed so much the lack of outdoor life that I had to be taken out of school. Just then it happened that my brothers, who had played a little tennis and taken to it enthusiastically, took me to San Rafael to see a match between the famous Sutton sisters, May and Florence; and we all decided then and there that this would be an excellent game for me. Since there was no available tennis court near us, our back yard with its gravel surface became our practicing place. This was in the summer of 1902.

I Learn to Keep the Ball in Play

Since the Suttons at that time played only from the back court, I had noticed that the ball crossed the net dozens of times before a point was scored and had made the obvious reflection that the game would be more interesting both to play and to watch if the ball were hit now and then before it bounced. When I questioned my brother Homer about it, he replied that men played more aggressively and soon after took me to see the Hardy brothers,

Sam and Sumner, in a doubles match. Both were quick and played at the net so that there was a lot of action, and I immediately tried to play the same way on our makeshift court in the back yard with a board for a net. In fact, because the gravel surface made the bound of the ball uncertain, I tried only to volley to keep the ball in play, which was more fun than having to hunt for it continually among the roses and berry bushes. We used to try to keep the ball going up to forty, fifty, or a hundred times before missing, and I had to develop alertness and balance in order not to miss.

Soon we found ourselves trying the same thing indoors, where, with the danger of a broken vase or lamp, there was even more crucial need of skill and accuracy, and I needed a quick wrist as well as perfect balance on my feet. A favorite practicing place outdoors was against the house between two lovely bay windows. When one of the boys broke a window, I feared my practicing was over, but an exception was made for me from the general ban and I was permitted to keep on banging against the house.

Most of my early practice was done in this way off a court, and ten or fifteen minutes at a time, but after a few months one of my brothers and I used to get up at half past five and run up to the court at the University of California a mile away, to get there before the crowd at six. Girls were not allowed to play after eight. The next year a neighbor, a friend of my father's, built a court and invited me to use it, so I did my piano practicing before breakfast to be free for tennis afternoons. Having a court we could use freely was like a gift from heaven.

My First Tournaments

My three older brothers, Miller, Homer, and Marius, were all much interested in the progress I was making, and I worked hard in response to their encouragement, so when they heard about a tournament for ladies in San Francisco on the Golden Gate Courts, I was duly entered. I met my partner in the doubles for the first time on the trip across the Bay from Berkeley, and we won the tournament, which was completed in one day. The following day the singles tournament was held and I was beaten in the final by the champion, Miss Varney. Having so much success in my first venture was a great encouragement, and what a lot I learned in those two days!

The next year I took part in handicap events played at Golden Gate Park and the following year was defeated in the State Tournament by Violet Sutton. In 1905 I went abroad with a friend and chaperon to visit in England and Scotland and played a lot of "garden tennis." We went down to Wimbledon, but to my lasting regret I did not enter and play there. On my return I played again in the Bay Counties Championships. When I entered the university the next year, I played there of course too, winning the championship each year and taking part in the intercollegiate events with Stanford, as well as in some outside tournaments. I was living in Berkeley still, but by this time we had a court of our own and my brothers were Bay Counties Doubles champions.

During the summer of 1908, I was allowed to go on the circuit of six or eight weeks of tournaments in the Pacific Northwest, a trip which proved very successful and very pleasant on account of the kind hospitality of the members of the various clubs. I have many happy memories of the circuit that year and the two following years, when I was welcomed by old friends in each place.

It happened quite frequently, then and since, that I was called on to play a man in an exhibition match. People always wanted to see how good I would be against a man. To their delight I usually won. The gallery seemed to be always with me, and the man so polite that he never played his best until I had quite a lead, which is what often happens in mixed singles. The man tries to exchange shots and does not feel called on to play his best game, usually a smashing game from the back court or the net, while the woman is playing the type of game at which she excels. I played the leading men players at that time, but in the twenty years since, except for Helen Wills, I have rarely heard of a woman playing in an exhibition match against a man.

In Tacoma, on one of these trips, I remember especially being entertained by Margaret Illington, who was married to one of my father's friends. The newspaper line about her at that time was that she had given up her career as an emotional actress to darn socks. We went to see Minnie Maddern Fiske in *Vanity Fair,* and I was much embarrassed to find that they had held the curtain for the arrival of our party.

The fall of 1908, when some eastern men came out to take part in the Pacific Coast Championships, was a turning point for me. George Wright, the veteran sportsman, brought his son Irving Wright, Nat Niles of Boston, and

Wallace Johnson of Philadelphia. They persuaded my mother to allow me to play in the National Championships in Philadelphia the following June, and Wallace Johnson invited me to play with him there in the mixed doubles. So when the time came, my father took me east.

National Championships

I shall never forget my excitement on arriving in Philadelphia and my dismay at the weather. It rained every day, making the courts difficult to play on at times. The number of grass courts impressed me greatly. I had seen some in the Northwest, but here was a whole field of them. Most of my matches were not very hard until I came to the finals, and then I had a close three-set match. It was in singles, and Louise Hammond was my opponent, playing a steady, heady game. The next day in the challenge round, I had a comparatively easy time with Mrs. Barger-Wallach, who had not been well. In those days the champion did not have to play through the tournament. Immediately following the singles came the ladies' doubles, and the mixed doubles, all played in the same afternoon. I finished at about half past five, and when I left at six on my train for the West, after being in Philadelphia less than a week, I could hardly realize that I had won all three events and was now the holder of three national titles.

A day or two after reaching home, I lost to May Sutton in an exhibition match at the old San Rafael asphalt court. It was a very hot day, and I well remember my blistered feet. In February there was a tournament at Coronado Beach, where she defeated me again. I played in the mixed doubles, however, with Maurice McLoughlin, and we won.

Maurice McLoughlin

One of the pleasantest associations of my tennis life has been my playing with Maurice, in practice and in tournaments. A more unselfish friend or more inspiring partner would be hard to imagine. He was always willing to come over from San Francisco and play on our court. We worked well together. I would give him dozens of lobs to smash, and he would do the same for me; then we would try long rallies, keeping the ball on each other's forehand or backhand. He was then perfecting his marvelous smash, one of the most effective and beautiful kills in tennis history. Of course I benefited in many ways and improved my game much sooner than I should have done otherwise. I was proud to be his partner, and the desire to continue to be good enough was a great spur to my ambition. I grew to know his game so well that when I watched him play I could often anticipate his tactics. Later, when he became an international figure, I probably felt as much joy in his successes and as much chagrin at his defeats as he did himself.

The Eastern Circuit

At Philadelphia in 1910, I successfully defended all three national titles, and the following year, when I went east after graduating from the University of California, I was allowed as a commencement present to stay and play in the other tournaments on the Eastern Circuit. After the National Tournament, in which I again won all three events, I played among other places at Longwood in Brookline and there met a slim young man, George Wightman, whom I was to marry the following year.

That was a memorable season for me in many ways. I won almost everywhere and at Niagara on the Lake played a match with May Sutton which is still remembered. After she had the first set 6-0 and was leading 4-1 on the second, I won the second 7-5 and the third 6-0. On the verge of defeat when she had four games on the second set, I suddenly said to myself, "That's no lead" — a phrase which has been long familiar to everyone I teach — and began to use my head. I realized that I was not getting down low enough to hit the balls in a way to lift them up, for the court was very wet. It was soggy when we began and kept getting worse because of the drizzle. As I steadied down I gained confidence and came through triumphant — in time to go to Newport to see Maurice McLoughlin play in the finals of the Men's National. His defeat by Larned is a tragic memory. Four years later I watched Maurice lose the National Singles. John McCormack, the singer, sat with me, and we were both in tears.

A Definite Objective

When I went back to California after that long season, I was tired but was persuaded to play in San Francisco. I remember the tournament because I did something I had never dreamed of being able to do, that is to go through with the loss of only one game to a match. It was a thrilling experience and came about through a chance remark. The first girl I defeated begged me not to let the next one get any more games than she had. So I made a special effort and held her to one game. Then I tried the same thing with the rest of my opponents, with a successful result that surprised me as much as anyone and that demonstrated to me for good and all the advantage of having a definite objective.

My recent acquaintance, George Wightman, meanwhile had an objective which brought him out of Harvard, graduating in February instead of June, and out to the West Coast. After a week's visit, my mother consented to our engagement. We were married soon after and made a leisurely trip east with his father and mother. And my tennis playing days were over for a time. There were tournaments that summer at Newport and New York, of course, and we attended, and there was plenty of tennis at Longwood, but I followed it all from a chair. My son George was born the following winter.

Back in the Game

When George was nine months old, however, I was back in the game and won at Longwood from Mary Brown in September, 1913. My husband and I won in the mixed doubles. Less than a year later my daughter Virginia was born, and we went to California to visit. On account of a sprained ankle I was on crutches a while and was unable to play until we returned to Brookline early in 1915. Then I had diphtheria, but I played in several tournaments that summer and was defeated only by Molla Bjurstedt. We took Molla with us when we went to California that fall to give the West a chance to see her. My daughter Hazel was born the next June and for a while I played very little.

My husband and I lost to Molla and Harry Johnson in the Fall Tournament at Longwood in 1916. Then came the war years, with my husband away at camp and exhibition matches to be played for the Red Cross. I played a great deal of "patriotic tennis" and in 1918 won the National Mixed Doubles with Irving Wright.

The next year in February I entered my first indoor national tournament, which was held at the Seventh Regiment Armory in New York. Somewhat to my surprise I came away with victory in the singles and in the ladies' doubles. That spring, too, I won the Metropolitan Singles Championship in New York, which I remember particularly because in the final match, I was behind one set and four games down before getting a game. Later on in Philadelphia it was fun to win the National Singles again just ten years after doing so for the first time. This was considered quite a feat.

Helen Wills

It was in 1920 that I first met Helen Wills. While visiting in Berkeley, I went to the club, where many children were playing, and discovered one girl with pigtails whose playing was outstanding. I asked immediately to meet her and we played several times together. Her physique and her concentration on the game were remarkable, and when I made suggestions, it was a delight to watch her immediate application of new ideas. A great desire to learn and an unswerving will to accomplish a definite job each day have been the chief reasons for her success. Always appreciative of her opponent, and unlike the average girl or boy of fourteen, who can seldom resist the temptation to waste time fooling on the tennis court, she played purposely from the beginning. She never played too long at a time, however, so that she was always very keen. No one could have had more pleasure than I in watching her progress to the position of premiere woman tennis player of the world. It was with me, I am proud to say, that she won her first three big doubles championships. Unspoiled by success, she is still the same charming girl she was when I first met her and, as all agree, is a great credit to America abroad and at home.

Indoor Tournaments

Because of illness, I was playing very little in 1920, but Wallace Johnson and I won the mixed doubles at Philadelphia for the third time, and I won the doubles in the women's national indoor tournament. The indoor tournament has been played in Boston since that year, and I have played in it regularly, winning the mixed doubles in '23, in '24 with Mr. Tilden, and in '26. In '27 I remember I had to my credit the ladies' doubles, the mixed doubles, and the singles — eighteen years after my first national championship. In '28 the mixed doubles and the ladies' fell to me again; and in '24 and '28, Helen Wills and I carried off the outdoor grass doubles.

Olympic Tennis

Our trip abroad in 1924 should go into the record too. Helen Wills, Eleanor Goss, Mrs. J. B. Jessup, Lillian Scharman, and I went to England with the rest of the Olympic team. The English ladies defeated us in the Wightman Cup matches, although Helen and I scored one victory in doubles. In Paris we did better, Helen winning the singles, both of us together the doubles, and R. Norris Williams and I the mixed doubles. Incidentally, tennis has not been included in the Olympic events since, so our titles all still hold! From Paris the team was invited to go to San Sebastian by the tennis club of that resort.

It was on this trip to San Sebastian, which Helen did not make, that I had the rare experience of playing with royalty. The Spanish royal family happened to be there visiting the Queen Mother. The American ambassador, Alexander Moore, called immediately when we arrived and brought an invitation from the queen to play the next day. So in the morning we went to the palace. I had some qualms as to the etiquette of the occasion, but there was no special ceremony. The queen put us at our ease immediately and we soon found ourselves with various members of the family starting for the courts in the royal gardens. We were going down the steps from the palace when the queen told me she was not going to play. She thought she was not good enough, but when I protested she called to one of her children as simply as any mother would, "Beatrice, go back and get my tennis shoes." So we played doubles, and the queen and Vinnie Richards won against me and my partner, Mr. Myrick, the captain of the men's team. When we had finished, the king remarked that it was very gracefully done, meaning that we had tossed the match. We had not done that exactly. They had won the points.

At the king's suggestion I then played against one of his nephews and his oldest son, the Prince of the Asturias, having for my partner Don Jaime, the second son. I would have done anything almost to win that match, it seemed to mean so much to the father and to Don Jaime, who was never on an equal footing physically with his brother. We did win, amid a good deal of teasing. It was a very natural family party, with the children sitting around on the grass and the king looking on and commenting with evident enjoyment. The Queen Mother was impressed when she heard that I had four children — my daughter Dorothy was a baby then. To both of us our families were more important than anything else in the world and we had a good time talking about them.

Back in America soon after, Helen Wills and I won the national outdoor doubles. I have had one more child since, my son William, who promises to become a sturdy athlete. I play off and on in local tournaments and am often asked to play in mixed doubles. In 1925 I played with Borotra, who had invited me a year ahead in England. The next year La Coste asked me. I have played with La Coste twice and each time we have been defeated in the finals. Sarah Palfrey and I won the ladies' indoor national championships four years in succession from 1928 on.

Great Women Players

During my years of tennis play there have been several dominant personalities among the women players. May Sutton was the first, then from 1915 on there was Molla Bjurstedt, for many years our national champion. Since then Helen Wills has been outstanding. In more recent years Sarah Palfrey has developed into the most sensational of younger players.

I first saw Sarah when she was eleven years old, and I marveled then at her perfect rhythm and timing. I have never seen her equal since. Her rise to the top of the fifteen-year-old class was rapid, and she easily headed the eighteen-year class for two years. She has had a handicap, however, in her physique. She has needed a few pounds to keep her nerves cushioned and also for reserve strength in hard matches. Because it is less wearing to play for fun and hard to study anything that comes to one so naturally, Sarah has neglected real competitive practice. To my mind it is important to have a definite plan in every match and to develop match temperament in that way. Perhaps since Sarah is known as my protégée, an analysis of her qualities as I see them will be helpful to other players.

I don't want to seem, in what follows, to disparage in the least her exceptional grace and natural rhythm. I would rather watch her on the tennis court, I think, than anyone else I have ever seen.

Sarah Palfrey

Sarah has always played well against me, as she still expects me to get everything, and she is on the alert for the best I can offer. In match play, on the other hand, she is often not ready for an opening when it comes. I have seen her defeat herself many times by missing simple setups through anxiety brought on by the strain of pulling out of too many tight places. If she were more rugged, the strain would not tell on her so much and she would be able to take the aggressive and maintain it throughout all her matches. Her doubles play has progressed better in the last few years because there, her natural quickness counts for more, and with a partner to help she is less anxious. The power of anticipation plays a big part in doubles, and hers has always been superb. Under less strain than in singles, she is able to relax and to exercise her natural skill.

Like many other players, Sarah needs to analyze her strokes more. Her lapses on the court are due to her unconscious assembling of energy and consequent lack of concentration on the shot at hand. When she was about fifteen her steadiness was uncanny and her return of service almost infallible. It was all play to her. But now she misses easy returns trying to make an ace with very little margin because she is more conscious of wanting to win the point and presses too soon on her shots on that account. The resulting errors cause her to be less relaxed and her natural rhythm is less dependable.

Another point which it may be profitable to others to note is that a few years ago she got into the habit of allowing the ball to drop very low before hitting it. This is dangerous because the margin for misjudging is too fine and many errors result. She now hits the ball much higher, thus getting more pace with less effort. It is easier to utilize the speed of an opponent's shot at a height where your body balance is even, and easier, too, to block a shot there in an emergency. If you plan to take a shot low and the ball comes faster than you expect, your return usually goes wild because your balance is not easy to adjust in the lower plane.

Sarah could play as well with everyone as she does with me if she would avoid unnecessary chances early in each game, so as to get the jump on her opponent. When serving, she should get her first serve in and should take the aggressive on the first return. When receiving, she should make her returns deep and away from her opponent so as to keep the advantage from the beginning. This would be less tiring and would conserve her strength for the later rallies. I have noticed also that she has kept her arm too low and too near her body on most forehand shots, which has caused many errors. The arms must be free and out from the body in order to rotate easily. On account of her natural grace and rhythm, she has not felt the need of care in stroking. These are not serious faults, however, when one is young and full of energy. Sarah is far superior to many girls who work much harder and is still the most fascinating and graceful young player on the courts.

Suzanne Lenglen

Among foreign women players, Suzanne Lenglen eclipsed everyone who preceded her and was the most colorful player of her time. I had one match with her in England, in 1924, and lost without getting a game, which has made me often wish that I could have played her again or when I was younger. It was a delight to have her for an opponent, though I am ashamed to say I suffered a bad case of stage fright playing in the center court at Wimbledon. Many games went to deuce and advantage and I would miss the game point by a small margin. She admitted exhaustion at the end of our match and said she would hate to play me again — which I considered a great compliment.

It has always seemed to me a great pity that she was ill when she came to America in 1922. I was in California at the time, playing often with Helen Jacobs, then a promising fourteen-year-old, but now our ranking woman player. I did see Suzanne at Wimbledon in 1924, however. She was obviously suffering in the last set of a long match with Miss Ryan, which she finally won. It took grit to keep on with defeat staring her in the face, and she proved herself a good sport. She was forced to default the next day and was forbidden by her doctor to play for a long time. From then on she was only a spectator at Wimbledon, but she was an ardent rooter for good shots and for her friends.

Suzanne excelled in agility and in anticipation of shots. On account of her natural grace her tennis was a joy to watch, and the accuracy of her shots seemed superhuman on account of the perfect control of her body at all times. She was the first person I had ever seen who used rhythm and balance to the utmost. She could summon speed with little effort but lacked tremendous power. Perfect rhythm gives unnoticed speed, but a girl tennis player needs to be sturdily built to get extreme speed without too costly an effort. For my part, I am a great believer in economy of motion. I find that it pays in the long run.

Teaching Children

Playing with children is its own reward. For years I have spent a great deal of my time coaching children and now and then running tournaments for them. In this activity I have been greatly aided by Mr. William S. Packer of Winchester, to whom I am greatly indebted, and whose help has encouraged me to attempt the children's tournaments as well as those for college girls in recent years. The work has been full of pleasure. At every successive visit to a school or playground, I see some result of my efforts that is gratifying. It may be evidenced only by the twinkle of an eye or a special smile from some shy child, or I may see an improvement in timing or anticipation. The field is infinite, and I make new discoveries continually. The naturalness of children and their response in unexpected ways give me endless enjoyment. My own tennis career, I strongly feel, would have been incomplete without this association with the younger generation.

It is a great pleasure to me, naturally, to read or hear of the success of one of my pupils. When I watch them, however, I have many anxious moments. It is more wearing than playing myself. I usually want the one who is playing better tennis to win, but sometimes I have been so divided in my minds as to suffer at mistakes on both sides. This is so exhausting that I have been forced of late to cultivate an indifferent attitude while the play is on.

Most of our good players in and around Boston I remember from their early junior days, and their progress has been a matter of pride and joy to me.

My playing with them, from the time when I lost only a few points until I began to lose games and finally sets, has been the best of entertainment to me. My plan has been to oppose them with a game of about the same difficulty so as to judge of their progress. As their games become better, however, I try not to give away sets. Every set has to be earned, though I have sometimes prolonged rallies and given setups to help confidence. I get real enjoyment from rallying with many different players and watching their increase in skill.

Advice for the Beginner

First of all it is important to choose clothes that are comfortable and permit freedom of movement for the arms, legs, and body. A narrow dress, for instance, can break the rhythm of stride and be an unnoticed cause of errors. Then supply yourself with light, flexible, rubber-soled shoes, which make starting, skipping, running, and stopping much easier than shoes of a heavier type. Then get a racquet which feels comfortable to hold as to handle and weight, and is evenly balanced. It is better to have a racquet too light than too heavy. Thirteen ounces — or even lighter for young children — is about right.

Now find a flat wall to bounce a ball against and familiarize yourself with the feel of the ball on the racquet. Just bouncing the ball on a sidewalk with a racquet by yourself, or to a friend, gives control and freedom in using this new implement. A very young child will instinctively take a grip suitable to the size of her hand and will develop every stroke quite naturally with enough practice.

Start your rallies gently and close to the bang-board with a shortened grip, and increase speed and depth as control of the ball comes. Try to keep the ball in play. This will develop anticipation and footwork. Count the number of times the ball is sent back and forth before missing. Set up an objective every time — for example, two forehands, then two backhands for five minutes — and stick to your plan. Have a definite object always as to placing and timing, and improve the number of rallies each day.

The ball should never be bounced in starting a rally. With the left foot kept on a line parallel to the direction which the ball is to take, place the right foot back diagonally towards the right side, not behind the left foot. Shift the body weight to the back foot, and have the right arm up, back, and out from the body. Then toss the ball up three feet or more, high enough to allow for your racquet, which has started up and farther back, to come back with the body weight and hit the ball alongside of you as the body weight is shifted to the front foot.

Any space or wall will do. If the floor or ground is smooth, let the ball bounce before returning it to the wall; if not, return the ball on the volley, choking the handle for short distances any time to avoid crowding, or hurrying the shot, or stepping away from the ball as you hit.

When you have hit hundreds of balls, you will probably have learned how important balance is and may never need to be told anything about footwork, which is the foundation of tennis as it is of most sports. But try to remember that every shot is made by first throwing the weight back onto your right foot for forehands, while keeping your back shoulder up and out, or onto your left foot for backhands. At the same time the racquet is tossed up and back with the left hand and left shoulder, then the body weight is thrown through the racquet onto the ball. All this is accomplished with perfect rhythm and timing after sufficient practice and gives any amount of speed desired. Girls who are graceful or who dance or skate learn the rhythm of tennis easily. Others can get it by working harder and may in the end apply it better. Remember in any case to keep your shoulder high, and your arms out, and to keep the head of the racquet up. It should rotate out and back in an oval loop which usually flattens on its forward motion toward the ball.

The best point at which to hit any ball is the one behind which you have perfect balance. Sometimes players prefer to hit the ball on the rise, sometimes on the top, or on the drop, as they have practiced doing one more than another. There is no one correct place, unless it is the highest point at which your balance can be well maintained. It is easier to lower your swing than to raise it, so it is safer to aim to hit all ground strokes about waist high. The variation comes naturally. To me it is difficult to control a ball on the rise as compared to the drop, or the top, but I find half-volleys a great aid in speeding up rallies or putting an opponent off her stride. In a half-volley, the ball is hit almost as soon as it strikes the ground. Every good player must be able to decide quickly which is the most advantageous point for any shot and be able to hit the ball there with perfect balance.

After each shot is made, a natural player will bring the racquet to rest with the throat in the left hand to have it ready to start on its backward toss when the body balance is ready for the next shot. If this is done, the muscles of the hitting hand will not tire or cramp in long matches and will respond to quick shots and angles more easily.

If you have been following these principles, you have realized already how easy it is to keep the ball in play, but you will still need much practice. As you become more skillful, when you rally with an inferior player, play your shots with a view to making it easy for your opponent to get the ball back. This gives you control. Refusing to play with inferior players, by the way, is short-sighted selfishness and does not make for the greatest enjoyment of the game. Personally I enjoy playing with good players and with poorer ones. When there has happened to be no good player available, I have been able to get much-needed practice from my children. It takes concentration, but that is a good thing for your game. To have to think not only of your own shot but of how to play and place it so that a return can be made helps to develop quick thinking and anticipation. Such practice is a kind of team play in which the partners are on opposite sides of the net helping each other.

Why Some Players Develop Faster

Some players have natural skill without proper application, and in others the situation is reversed. Just as in schoolwork, pupils learn more quickly where inclination and application are combined. Perhaps one player is deterred because there is no time or place available for practice on a court, while another gets practice using a side wall or a barn door. Tennis is easier for the girl who has a background of activity in other sports — the more the better; and if she has ambition to learn the fundamental principles and to practice, she will develop faster than others who have natural ability but no interest in principles.

As in almost everything in life, brain power is necessary. I can think of numbers of players who might be termed stylists, who have pretty strokes, but who have little success against a change-of-pace game. Their own game is obvious and easy to break up. They have practiced hitting every ball on either side at about the same height and speed and can beat the average player who tries doing the same thing without the hours of practice. On the other hand, a player who is quick to note weaknesses in an opponent and who knows how to utilize balance and rhythm in her own strokes will improve rapidly because she will be able to vary her shots quickly in emergencies. She will not try to play the same game against everyone but will do what is necessary to upset her opponent, and in that way will gain confidence herself.

A player with knowledge of the when, how, and why of shots is seldom an "in and outer," because as soon as she realizes she is getting her shots out she knows what to do to get them in. She does not say, "My forehand just won't go in today!" but is able to bring out her best tennis when required. No one can rise to great heights every day, it goes without saying, and there are exceptions due to nervousness or a much superior opponent, but a knowledge of fundamentals and of the psychology of the game will do a great deal towards winning from a better but unthinking player.

Although you should play as well as you can under all circumstances, never try to do better than you know how. This is often the reason an inferior player is swept off the court. She will spend most of the match trying to outplay an opponent who is ready for every move instead of playing the game as she can best play it. I often encounter this type when teaching. Their aim seems to be to score an unorthodox ace against me, with the result that they get much less practice than others who wait for an opening after long rallies. There is nothing better for footwork and anticipation than the opportunity to make dozens of different strokes in rapid succession.

When I give the average medium player a great many lobs, I can see her confidence in hitting overhead shots develop almost immediately. It is more difficult to get quick results from practice on ground strokes as the bounce of the ball as well as the surfaces of courts vary so much that accurate judgment of the exact point to strike the ball is not easy to acquire. Some players think quickly; some act quickly. The ideal player, of course, must do both.

Strokes

Teachers and writers about tennis would make the principles easier to grasp and apply if they would stress the point that balance and rhythm are the foundation of every shot. A slight skip or a step gives momentum, which is obviously harder to gain from a stationary position; and rhythm is developed through skipping and shifting of weight. Here is a simple method for making most strokes. Of course, these directions should be reversed for left-handed players.

While waiting for any shot, the body must be erect, with the shoulders up and the arms out. Shifting the weight is uniform then, as the shoulders carry their share and do not need another motion to be in position for the shot. If the ball is coming on your right, put your weight on your right foot, with your right shoulder and elbow up and out from your body, not behind it, so that when the ball has almost hit the ground, your racquet gets its final toss back with a push from the left foot and left hand and travels well up and out in time to get its forward push for the shot from the right foot.

Few players do all this. There are three types: those who make each stroke with the initial push from the back foot, those who start the shot by pivoting the muscles of the center of the body, and those who use only the right shoulder and the right arm. The first way is the best one, and the easiest, too. If it is necessary to check shots or add speed by using the middle muscles of the body or of the arm as well, little more effort is required to do so. I often compare this use of the muscles to the use of the two brakes on an automobile. The push from the back foot is to be used as a regular thing, while the pivoting of the upper part of the body is like the emergency brake, to be used only when there is special need. Many players, even some good ones, transgress in this respect and take liberties with their balance, which makes it easy to account for their defeats.

If the ball is to be returned on your left side, the body weight should shift to the left foot, and the left shoulder and elbow should go up and out from the body. This gives your right arm room to go back free from your body and keeps the head of the racquet up. The left hand should always support the racquet at its throat until the ball has bounced. In this position you are ready to block a hard shot or to make any type of shot there is time for. You can move forward or back or further to the left with little effort and still have your racquet ready. Control of the shot is gained for the most part by getting the back shoulder high and the arm out from the body before the forward motion is begun. Speed depends on the amount of push from the back foot and the pull of the top part of the body just before the ball is hit. Pace is usually determined by the amount of spin, slice, or top imparted to the ball by the racquet at the moment of contact.

One should learn to play with a minimum of fatigue rather than with maximum speed, for reserve strength may be needed in a long match. It is better to acquire a speed that can be used with economy of strength, and with balance rather than strain, with versatility rather than violence. A swift shot that goes out only benefits one's opponent. So control is to be desired more than speed. Start gently controlling the ball, and work up to speed.

With practice one can learn to execute any kind of shot by keeping in mind that the racquet head must be out from the body in time to make the desired shot without hurrying. Try to be ready and waiting to stroke, rather than arriving and stroking at the same time. And remember that every ball should be hit out to the side before the weight has shifted to the front foot. The left hand and shoulder should always start the backward swing of the racquet as the weight is being shifted to the right foot for forehand shots, with the right arm and shoulder out and high. The muscles and shoulder of the right arm are not needed until the forward swing. Get your weight onto the back foot before removing your left hand. In forehands, the right foot starts the forward swing, with the right arm well out diagonally back to the side of the body for all backcourt play. For the volley there is less of a swing of the racquet back and forward. Do not step onto the front foot. Just throw or shift the weight onto it. The back foot, or pushing foot, should be well behind the ball before the shot is even begun. It is much easier to control the rhythm of your body when the hitting foot is well behind the place where the ball hits the ground. Timing depends on the distance and speed of the shot. When the distance is long, preparation and stroking are slower than in the case of short distances. Recovery should be relatively quick after any shot, and especially so after short ones. Getting to the proper position to hit again should be as rapid as possible so that the stroking need not be hurried. Make shorter swings at close range so as to recover more quickly, and keep the shoulders and the arms well up and the balance on the balls of the feet for quick shifts of weight. Choking the handle of the racquet also when at close range will help you to be ready for the next return. It is not necessary to keep your hand up the handle when you make the shot unless the ball is fast and close to you. But it will aid your posture to do so in preparation for any shot, as your shoulder will be kept high and free when your two hands are nearer together on the racquet, the left hand at the throat and the right hand up from the end.

The Forehand

Stand erect, with the racquet held lightly near the end by the right hand, and at the throat by the thumb and forefinger of the left hand. Step back diagonally to the right onto the ball of the right foot. Keep the left foot in the line of direction of the shot and the right shoulder and elbow up and out. The left hand supports the racquet head and carries it well out from the body. As soon as it releases the racquet, the left hand should be carried on farther back by the natural rhythm of the body and then should follow the motion of the body in the stroke, acting as a balance, until the racquet comes back to rest in it again. The left hand and arm should never hang down by your side during any stroke but should move in a plane well above the waist for most shots. For very low shots, both arms are lower. The left is somewhat lower than the right on all forehand shots.

Still pictures can hardly tell the story when motion is being represented — even motion pictures in the flat are often misleading — but I am including a few to help make these instructions clear. If you will study them, racquet in hand, you can make your own motion pictures. For the forehand, get yourself into position No. 1, with your right arm and racquet well up, out, and back to your right side, then, as in No. 2, push with your right foot, and as the momentum travels up through the body your racquet will come in contact with the ball, as in No. 3, with a very slight added impetus from the right shoulder and arm. Complete the rhythm of your swing and return as nearly as possible to the position in No. 4. If the shot is lightly hit, the arc of the swing and follow-through is smaller.

Try this motion gently at first, without a ball, keeping the arms free and the shoulders well back, then increase your speed. If you can get a space large enough in front of a mirror, try it there and see if you are doing what you think you are. Repeat it many times, then take a skip first each time and see how naturally you will fall into the rhythm of it. From this simple exercise you can develop many different ways of hitting successfully once you have learned the principle of transferring the weight of your body onto the ball. In actual play, of course, there may be times when your feet will be differently placed and you will take liberties with the coordination of your legs and body, but this is not desirable as a regular habit because the errors are too costly. Many good players would be better still if they would give more attention to their footwork with relation to their shoulders.

The Backhand

Stand erect, as for the forehand, with the racquet held lightly near the end by the right hand, and at the throat by the thumb and forefinger of the left hand. Step back diagonally to your left onto the ball of your left foot so that your feet are in the line of direction of the shot. Keep your left shoulder and elbow high and out from the body. Then allow your right arm and elbow to swing around to the left, low and out, and release the left hand as you shift your weight, but do not drop it. It follows out and back to gain momentum as the body weight is carried back farther just before the forward push. Then it follows the flight of the racquet and is ready to take the racquet's weight after the shot.

Right here, though it may seem repetitious, I should like to stress again the importance of the left arm for rhythm and balance. This is something not sufficiently realized. I am always seeing beginners taught tennis in a one-armed way. Pupils are allowed to hang the left arm limply down while making the back and forward swing with the right arm alone. The left as well as the right arm and elbow must be held up and free from the body at all times. This makes starting to either side, backward or forward, very simple because the shoulders do their share in lifting the weight and allowing the upper part of the body to be pivoted freely. The back shoulder must be higher than the front shoulder in making all shots; and for low shots or high, the shoulders have the same relative position. Though sometimes slower or faster, sometimes higher or lower, the preparation for a stroke is always the same.

The Serve and the Smash

It should be kept well in mind that a serve, smash, drive, drop shot, chop, cut, volley, or half-volley all have the same basis of balance and rhythm and are made by throwing the weight onto the back foot, then onto the front foot as the ball is hit. This is a simple principle to teach and to learn as compared to technical elaborations and descriptions of grips, stiff wrists, follow-through, and other details too involved for beginners. Without first acquiring rhythm, it is a hard task to learn to play.

"Keep your shoulder down!" teachers say, or "Step into it!" though I am sure the pupil would find it easier if the advice were, "Shoulders up and back!" and, "Throw your weight in the direction of the shot!" It is necessary to have the shoulders up and the arms out from the body to make weight-shifting easy and to avoid pulling shots with your shoulder. In running or moving about, too, the shoulders should carry the top part of the body so that the shifting of the upper part of the body becomes automatic according to the position of the feet. Players who do this are light on their feet and move with less effort so that they expend less energy in play.

To serve, stand back of the service line with the shoulders and racquet well up and the feet in a line with the direction the ball is to take. Then to gain momentum for the actual hitting, the weight is thrown onto the back foot while the arms work automatically, throwing the ball up and the racquet up and back. While the ball is going up, the head of the racquet has time to drop back in a way similar to the back swing with an Indian club. A light spring with the back foot is then necessary to start the shift. The racquet must go up first before going forward against the ball, which should be hit before the front foot takes the weight. If the ball is thrown high — and I mean high, four or five feet at least above your head — on an imaginary line up between your feet, you will quickly develop a dependable serve.

Later, when you have better control, you can develop variations. There are many ways to do so. Watch a few players and you will be surprised at the differences. The feet will be placed in various directions and will sometimes be moved. The ball and racquet will be thrown at different angles. But if you watch carefully from the beginning to the end, you will discover the fundamental body-shifting, which has perhaps been developed after a great deal of practice. The best way for a beginner is the one that is simplest to control.

The hitting plane for serving is higher than for any other shot except the smash, which should be identical as to the actual hitting motion. Since the stance is not stationary as in serving, the smash is perhaps the most beautiful of shots. The height of the ball makes the rhythm more pronounced. Get someone to toss up lobs by the dozen, and place every shot as you return them until you work up gradually to an ace. Accuracy and timing become easy with plenty of practice.

The serve is like the other strokes except that you have to start the ball with your left hand and so must gain momentum in a high plane with your racquet supported only by your right hand. The best way to hold the racquet is the one which seems the most natural and comfortable when you hit. This is usually with the flat side of the handle against the palm of your hand. Swing the racquet up and far back so as to get plenty of momentum and toss the ball high enough to give plenty of time to hit with perfect balance before your weight is shifted to the front toes.

Foot faults can be avoided by keeping the toes of the left foot on the ground and not swinging the other foot through until after hitting the ball. A foot fault is an infringement of the rules and should be considered cheating, but many players are careless in this respect. The server who rushes to the net gains an advantage by being a step nearer, but in the long run, I think the foot-faulters gain nothing but a bad reputation. I still hope for the day when this infringement will be rare and there will be no need of a foot-fault judge.

The Drive

Driving is the usual method of exchange of shots and is made with the same shifting of weight whether the shot is backhand or forehand. The safest place to hit the ball is about waist high and, as I have already said, just as the weight is being transferred to the front foot. Always have the right shoulder high and free so that the right arm with the racquet will go up and out automatically as you move to the right. The left hand must hold the racquet at the throat.

When the right foot is at its final place, then the right arm with the racquet will continue on back and out and the momentum for the forward swing will come from the push by the right foot. This push eliminates the need of pulling with the shoulder and arm and tends to give perfect balance, as it distributes the power behind each shot and allows the top part of the body plenty of leeway for change of direction or speed before the weight reaches the front foot. A few players start the forward swing with the muscles around the waistline and throw the front foot across so as to catch the weight of the pivoting shot before reaching too far across the body; but beginners should not try this, as it is difficult form to use with accuracy, besides being wearing and not adaptable for all shots. Even for experienced players it is hard to handle change of pace and bad bounces with this motion. The margin for shifting balance is too slight, so that errors usually result.

The Volley

Volleying should be practiced early, as good footwork there is absolutely essential, and it is easier to learn to volley in the beginning before you have become accustomed to play from the backcourt where you have more time between shots. It is easy to go from fast play to slow play.

The foundation is the same as in ground strokes, but it is even more important to have the racquet rested in the left hand between shots, as the swing back and forward is shorter, and the hitting muscles need to be fresh for the greater demands made on them. There is more snap and wrist motion in the volley, and the body is used to a lesser degree. Do not hurry any shot, but especially not a volley. Get your balance and hit from the back foot as usual, never reaching out for the ball. Hit the ball before your body weight shifts — and pivot with it. The hitting plane is higher than for most ground shots, so the back shoulder must be kept up and free for quick shifting or rotating of the body. The shoulders must be ready earlier than for back-court play because of the shorter distance from your opponent.

There is almost as great a variety of grips as there is of racquets, and no one is the correct one. Some players place the thumb up the handle on backhand shots, but I have yet to see perfect volleyers do so. It works well for back-court play, and many good players use the thumb in that way, but I do not advise it as a general practice. It is wiser to use practically the same grip for all shots on the backhand, whether on the volley or bounce. Some players use the same side of the racquet for backhand as for forehand shots; others use both sides. The grip when hitting is practically the same either way, though moving the head of the racquet is different. The backward swing, which is always started with the left hand at the throat of the racquet, is made easier by using the same side and keeping the face of the hitting side toward the ball for both forehand and backhand shots. The grip is slightly changed as the racquet is shifted from one side to the other. The right hand should be relaxed anyway after each shot, and a fresh grip taken each time. If the same side of the racquet is used, the shift of grip comes while the head of the racquet is higher.

The right hand should always be loosened as soon as the racquet head returns to the left-hand thumb and forefinger. The slight shift in grip then comes automatically with the shift in body weight.

Balance and Rhythm

Balance, or the lack of it, is evidenced in every point played. Playing on different surfaces or in the wind can be done with accuracy when the balance is perfect, enabling one to skip quickly and easily to adjust oneself to a change in the flight or bounce of the ball. Perfect balance and rhythm are to be striven for at all times. Though some good players take liberties in the matter of footwork and balance after years of play, they are not to be imitated. If you find you have lunged for a shot, make a special effort not to the next time, and you will soon learn how to get there with an extra skip and pivot, and with time to spare.

Never stand flatfooted. It is hard to start quickly that way. But when the weight of the body is on the ball of one foot, it is easy to shift it to the other one to make a start in the right direction. Never lunge to any position. Skip instead, and hold the racquet up and back, which will give you more time to hit the ball with proper balance, as the head of the racquet gets back sooner that way. Start the instant your opponent hits the ball — or before — so as to be in a position where the racquet head can be as nearly as possible behind the ball in the line of its flight before it is time for the forward swing. Then hit only as hard as the body balance can stand. Accuracy is essential and can only be obtained by perfect rhythm and timing. Anticipate changes of speed. Your ears should help you there. I am always conscious of the different sounds of shots. Then be ready as quickly as possible for timing each shot properly.

The real essentials of successful tennis playing — I can hardly say it too often — are balance and rhythm. But balance and rhythm and the coordination of the muscles necessary to time and hit a ball come usually only with practice, determination, and perseverance. Observation of good players is a help, but one has to learn what to observe first. Watch the player, her footwork, her arms, shoulders, and the flight of her racquet. Nothing is gained by watching the ball when not playing. The player, of course, watches the ball from the time it leaves her opponent's racquet until she hits it, then she watches her opponent until the ball is hit again.

Some players hit a great many balls off balance and wonder why they miss shots. On the other hand, many good players make lucky shots when a ball hits the wood or off center on the racquet but goes inside the court because their body balance was right. These shots, of course, are not just due to luck but are the result of correct preparation. A skip just before making a shot is a good way to insure perfect balance. And there are times when a couple of skips will do what a step or run cannot do. Moving backward and sidewise as well as frontward with perfect balance is essential. This is helped by holding the arms up and away from the body. Always keep in mind that the shoulders follow the feet. If your right foot is back your right shoulder should be up and back, and the same applies to the left foot and shoulder. Of course, perfect accuracy is unattainable, but a high degree of accuracy can be obtained by having perfect balance before starting any stroke. If a ball strikes a rough spot or you slip, it is easy then to meet the emergency. Perfect balance on the feet gives perfect control of the weight for a spring or jump or sudden shift if the ball bounds in an unexpected direction. And the knees are very important. Have them ready for the skip or spring.

Shoulders

I cannot stress too often the importance of well-balanced shoulders. Some teachers tell pupils to drop their shoulders and let the arms hang freely while waiting for a shot. This only prolongs the time necessary to learn control of all shots because it hampers the natural swing and rhythm of the body and requires more effort for each stroke. Any young person just starting will learn twice as quickly if encouraged to keep her shoulders up and ready to follow the feet in a higher plane. The top of a suspension bridge holds up the weight of the bridge. In the same way your shoulders can lift part of your body weight and make you lighter on your feet. For a volley or net game or good serving or smashing, high shoulders are absolutely necessary. Even good players are apt to take liberties with their shoulder position and should check up occasionally on this point.

Try to be waiting to hit the ball rather than just getting into position at the last second. You can then have your weight ready to throw onto your racquet as it hits the ball. Perfect balance, with the feet placed in the line of direction of the shot, will enable you to put your weight behind the stroke at the proper angle, the proper time, and the proper place.

Position on the Court

The first position on the court when receiving the serve is near the baseline at the point where you expect the server to aim. In doubles the center of your territory is the place to be, but it changes rapidly and often. You should always be at the baseline or back of it for ground strokes. For volleys you should be halfway between the net and the service line or nearer for short ones.

If a player has a hard, deep serve, stand well back of the baseline, as the greater distance gives more time to get in position to return a fast ball. Try to be in the line of direction from which the ball is coming. It is a great advantage, of course, to return some serves with a drop shot just over the net. To do this, stand as near the service line as possible in order to shorten the distance the ball has to travel and the time the opponent has to reach it. Be alert and flexible in your mind as to the best position, and try out different places when practicing to find out the most advantageous position for different types of serves. Do not let your opponent suspect what you are going to do, however, or you may get caught in the wrong place.

After serving, one should get as near the center of the court near the baseline as possible, and be prepared to go to the spot where the return is coming. By watching the opponent carefully, one can often tell where the ball is to be placed and can get a very quick start in the right direction. Aggressive, decisive returns will enable you to get to the net position, which is approximately on the center line halfway between the net and the service line. From there it is easy to go nearer the net for hard volleys and back for high shots, but one should always return immediately to the home position. Never stay on the deadline, which is about at the service line, where, except for high volleys, it is hard to hit any ball accurately. Many players get caught there when a step or two up or back would have saved them.

Tactics

In rallying before a match, always size up your opponent. Give her plenty of chances to hit every kind of ball and watch her reaction to each one. Warm up slowly. Never begin by banging everything as hard as possible, but get confidence in the very beginning with control of your shots. And give your muscles a chance to get warmed up before taxing them.

When you begin to play, concentrate continually so that you get an early lead. This will give you confidence and enable you to play better and will usually have the opposite effect on your opponent. When you get the first point, the business at hand is to get the second. Then, do not relax, as many do when they are ahead, but make the most of the situation, and keep the ball in play with more of a margin of safety. Give your opponent an opportunity to miss. She will seldom take chances when you lead by two or three points so will give you another shot to force her on. Three returns will usually win the point when your opponent is behind and worried about the situation. Still, many a match has been lost when a player had a commanding lead and began pressing shots, trying to make them more decisive, when they were already forcing enough. The errors then gave the opponent confidence. You will not find it hard to concentrate in a pinch if you have formed the habit of having a special place for every shot. It will take you some time to learn where they can be placed most effectively, but never hit idly. If you do you are likely to find yourself in trouble or being pressed and that it is too late to get the upper hand.

There is no value in a serve that is swift but out of court; so place your serve well on your opponent's backhand and don't try an ace unless you have control. Much strength is wasted on unsuccessful attempts to make an ace. Your opponent should be kept on the defensive by your next shot, which should be one she has to run for, then you can usually score with the next shot. It seldom takes more than three shots to win a point if your first serve has put your opponent on the defensive from the beginning. Serving without a plan is apt to put you on the defensive instead and to give your opponent a chance to win the point with one or three shots. Have a definite plan of attack at every stage.

When receiving, try to place your return of service so as to make your opponent step up to reach the ball. A deep shot on her backhand is usually the best to try for. The next return should then be deep and well over on the other side of the court. Then you should be ready to score the winning shot. Take care not to make an error at this stage or your good work will have gone for nothing. And be quick to anticipate the opening. It may not come until there have been many exchanges over the net, but if you are ready and alert, the kill will be easy. If you have the least doubt about your balance, allow more margin towards the center of the court as well as over the net. In case of a difficult serve, try to anticipate it and get your racquet behind where the ball is going to bounce. Then it is easy to block the ball and take its speed instead of stroking it. To block a ball, get the racquet head out and parallel to the net, push your body weight from the back foot even more firmly than for other shots, and avoid pulling with your hitting shoulder.

I have played some people who regularly fail to return the third ball in a rally and do not attempt an aggressive shot. My plan of campaign against them is very simple. I play three or four safe returns deep in court and the match is won. Others are "four or five shotters." Others still become aggressive on the second, third, or fourth returns, so I attack them with my first or second shot before they get their stride. With others who are so aggressive on the first shot that it is hard to reach, I return the shot deep and high to give myself more time to reach the next one.

Angles

Angles in tennis are very difficult for some people to play. They should be studied in various games, such as billiards, squash, and Crokinole, to understand the finer points. On a tennis court the angles are wider because of greater distances and have to be judged accordingly. A wonderful way to learn about them is to begin by aiming a shot near the center of the court, and then aim one a little farther over, then one still nearer the sideline. Try to determine the best place for your feet each time, and try the same thing with harder shots.

When playing at the net it is best to volley the first ball deep and straight, unless you are perfectly set for it. Angle the second one if you are in good position, waiting to hit. It is always easier, by the way, to volley a ball in the direction from which it has come, unless you are perfectly set for an angle or kill shot. Always avoid hurrying the shot, and angle less acutely from an angle. The speed of the shot must be taken into account too. It is safer to return hard shots with less of an angle because of the tendency the angle then has of becoming less accurate.

Your opponent must either be outplayed or kept from playing her best game. Respect her ability. If you expect each shot to be returned, you will not be caught flatfooted. But try to be a shot ahead of the game by maneuvering her into giving you a setup on your next shot, and watch her as soon as you have hit the ball to get a jump ahead by anticipating her return. Even if it seems hopeless to win a point by playing a shot, try it, for there is a chance of succeeding and your opponent might miss on the return. So play your luck! And try to make the right guess as to your best position to prevent an ace. The tide has been turned many a time by such a return. In a close rally, toss up a lob to upset your opponent. Any return is better than a miss.

Very often you can trick your opponent into playing a shot into a space which seems wide and unprotected, but which you have guarded. If this is done now and then, it has a very demoralizing effect and will win many points for you. It will cause your opponent to lose her poise and a subsequent point or two because she will be disconcerted at the loss of an apparent setup. This is yet another reason for returning a shot even though it has to be right into the opponent's hands.

Watch for advantage continually by taking note of your opponent and her mental reactions. When something annoys her, then is the time for extreme care on your part. I have seen a fine player defeated by a clever opponent who only used a semi-lob shot; it annoyed her so much that she could not handle it calmly. Lack of mental control is a big factor in lack of shot control. It works for or against you as the case may be. Get control of every situation as quickly as possible. The quick action mentally may give you the lead you need to overcome some adversaries. When you see your opponent hesitate, decide what the cause is and use it to good advantage. When you are behind in the score, try being a little more aggressive and eliminate all possibility of errors.

When you are leading, you can safely be less aggressive, but do not change an already winning game.

Mixed shots will puzzle your opponent; so versatility is worth striving for, though it involves more work that simply practicing one type of forehand and backhand. If you learn to play all kinds of shots, you will have them to call on at the psychological time to baffle your opponent. A quick, snappy volley speeds up play. A slice or topspin is disconcerting to many and can be used to advantage almost any time. Use whatever shot will keep your opponent at her worst. When a player is not well accustomed to slices or cuts, or cannot anticipate certain spins accurately, she will often hurry her shot and make an error. Never be too sure, however; she may learn quickly what to do, and you will need to change your tactics.

Returns

Remember that successful returns must be over the net and inside your opponent's court. Your first return in any game should be more defensive than other shots in order to get the range early. By defensive I mean not too hard, with plenty of margin over the net, and not too near the lines. Vary your direction each time so that your opponent has to guess where it is going. A deep, slow ball to the forehand corner has the advantage of giving you time to be ready for the return, while a fast one leaves your left court open for a fast passing shot. A slow, high, deep shot to the middle of the court will often bring an easy return and give you a chance immediately for a winning shot. A fast, hard shot right at your opponent might give her an ace on you before you can get set for the return. A slow, deep shot to your opponent's left side will give you time to get into position for a forcing shot on the next return, when a hard, deep one may catch you out of position. If you can vary your first returns with a deep chop or cut stroke occasionally, it will be very helpful. After the rally is on, then work up to more speed and deception in your shots. The best players are the ones who can vary their shots as to direction and speed. A young player who literally knocks the cover off the ball at each shot usually defeats herself. A clever opponent will take speed from her shots and find it less wearing than forcing the shots herself.

Mental Attitude

There is as much to the mental side of tennis as there is to the manner of making shots. Your general mental attitude is very important. Cultivate a buoyant spirit, and remember the game's the thing. You should enjoy every phase and should never hesitate to be natural. Show admiration for your opponent's skill if you like, but control expressions of displeasure. Some players are naturally more demonstrative than others, but it is as important to control yourself as it is to control the ball. If you make an error, you should be able to analyze it coolly and at least keep a calm exterior. Do not think about it too long. Put your mind on the next shot, and on how you can better your situation.

It is important to analyze your good shots, too. In fact, you should give thought to every detail of the game. You may not be able to cope with them all. Your sense of proportion will have to help you there. And try to be extremely charitable. It pays in the long run, even though you may lose several matches en route. The best solution of difficulties is in constructive thinking about your own game. Never make the excuse that "nothing goes in today," or that you "don't know what is wrong" with your forehand or backhand. Your feet may have been poorly placed, you may not have gotten your racquet back far enough, or you may have brought it back too late, or perhaps you hurried the shot, or hit the ball too high or too low. Your shoulders may have been down so that you were moving with effort and hurrying your shots.

Don't Defeat Yourself

If your opponent's cuts, chops, lobs, or soft shots bother you, concentrate on getting the returns in court and not on how much you dislike the game against you. Most players defeat themselves, so try not to help your opponent that way. Make your own shots such that she will be bewildered and bothered first. And never let small annoyances disconcert you. A child's crying, a train or a fire engine passing are reasons sometimes given for defeats. But if the player had paid strict attention to keeping the ball in play, the result would have been better. No sprinkler nor steamroller will have power to bother you if you concentrate on the business at hand.

In a pinch, call on your courage instead of worrying. Persons who have practiced with me are very familiar with certain expressions I have found helpful, such as "Forty love is no lead," or "Our game," "Two to three — nearly three all," or "Give up!" at 5-2 for instance, and other jocular battle cries. Players who are used to joking in practice can often come through a close match because they know the value of relaxation in a tight place. They have learned to smile under adverse circumstances.

It's an Ill Wind

Most experiences can be turned to good account. I remember several which were slight in themselves but which have affected my game for the better. Early in my career, for instance, an opponent showed great annoyance at a cut stroke and implied that it was cheating to make such a shot. I gave it some thought and decided that a reliable stroke of that kind would be very useful against certain players. Since then I have used a chop almost entirely on the return of service, as most players are unable to make an aggressive return from the different twists I can impart to the ball.

Again, a player during our warming up before a match used to place all her returns so that I got almost no practice at all. This was done innocently, but it is an unsportsmanlike thing to do. It is better to try a placement after several exchanges, when each one has had plenty of warming up. I used to spend the entire five or ten minutes picking up balls and had to plan to rally beforehand with a friend. When I thought about it, I realized that the more shots I gave an opponent to hit, the more I learned about her good and bad points, with the result that I have always tried to make my own rallying very steady.

I remember another incident which upset me but which also taught me something. A girl I played with had a habit of throwing her racquet into the back net after losing one of our long rallies. Then she would saunter leisurely back to pick it up, causing quite an interval before play could be resumed. This annoyed me, as my game went better without the long waits. But I learned to take a much-needed breathing spell — almost peaceably, if not quite.

Doubles

It rarely happens that two fine singles players make an equally fine doubles team. This is due to lack of cooperation and also to the necessity for faster and more decisive thinking in doubles than in singles. On account of the sudden changes it is necessary to think and act almost simultaneously, and sometimes you must speak as well. Some can only develop this quick thinking after long practice. But in America, where our distances are so great, it has been difficult for the best men as well as the best women to practice much in doubles as a team.

Good teamwork requires an understanding of tactics and combined position play, and certainty as to which one should play each shot. It is easy to develop all this if you play a great deal with one partner. Each player should take the responsibility for her own shots and should give information quickly if she is not going to play the next one. Some doubles players have a tendency to relax as soon as they have made a shot, and for that reason they often get caught out of position. I make it a practice myself to follow the play closely on every shot. If it is not my shot my activity makes it easy to give quick information. A perfect doubles combination is impossible without constant cooperation. In spite of this, some players play a "solo" game, leaving their partners frequently in doubt as to their tactics, with a resulting indecision that is disastrous. I have even known a player to ask her partner to keep quiet, though information was proving most necessary. This alone showed poor cooperation, and the team was weakened by it.

A simple rule and a very important one is that you should watch your opponents when your partner is serving or returning a shot. Though it is very natural to do so, you should not turn to keep your eye on a ball after it has crossed the net to your side. If it is not your shot, turning to follow the ball is apt to get you off balance for the next return, which may be coming to you. Face the front as much as you can, especially when the rallies are fast. Anticipation on any shot comes from watching your opponent prepare for it, so be watching her as early as possible.

Information in Doubles

Obviously the two most important things in doubles are cooperation and information. A poor partner who cooperates is better than a more skillful player who attempts hard shots at the wrong time and causes her partner to get caught out of position. Frequent information will prevent misunderstandings. There should be no doubt about "ins" and "outs" and whose shot it is. Quiet calling during rallies makes for better teams. If you are used to saying "Mine," "Yours," or "I have it," there will be less chance of a panicky shout in a crisis and the consequent loss of a point or a game. The person who has just played a ball is better able to judge the return and should have the responsibility of either playing or calling the next shot if it is close, unless her partner calls or steps in ahead to play it.

Fewer chances should be taken on returns of service in doubles, so they should be made defensively, unless it is possible to make a safe ace. A deep return to the server will do no harm, while a short shot or lob or a hard drive to the net player may put your partner at a great disadvantage. There should be a greater margin of safety than in singles. Do not at any time take a chance that will put your partner under fire. Make your returns all well away from your opponents so that your partner will not get caught. If you think there is a chance for an ace, place it so that a possible return will come to you rather than to your partner.

Strategy in Doubles

One has to work harder mentally in doubles because there are more possibilities of plays, and more need of quick thinking. And strategy cannot be so well worked out in advance because the scene shifts constantly. So work with your partner, giving information as early as possible and being ready to call or play on every shot. It does no good to try to make a shot when off balance. It is better to leave it to your partner on the chance that she may have anticipated its location, so just call "Yours" quietly. Your information should be given just as the ball is hit by your opponent, not when the ball is about to be played on your side.

A good way to save time and energy any time on a court is to keep track of the balls and have them handy when you are serving and near your opponent when she is serving. In doubles, with very little care your partner can always have an extra ball in her hand for you. Whenever an opponent misses a shot near a line on your side, be sure to call out so that your partner understands. It is disconcerting to have to guess or ask about a shot. Be sure always, if there is a doubt, to play the shot over. In doubles your partner should watch all close serves and line shots and be able to give a prompt decision.

Change of pace is as effective in doubles as it is in singles. When a player is stroking and timing everything accurately, change your speed and the height of your returns. This will often put her off and give you quite a lead before she realizes what is happening. In doubles or singles, be adaptable and give up an unsuccessful plan. Avoid piling up errors because something is not working as you expected. This is the time to say to yourself, "Over, not in the net," "Inside, not outside of court." Just get your returns in, deep and high if necessary, and you will soon strike your stride again.

Anything which causes your opponent to be puzzled or out of position works well for your side. For instance, deep shots keep your opponents in the back court and put them on the defensive, giving your side the upper hand if you are both ready to take the net. It is important that both of you should be ready for the opening when it comes, because if either hesitates the advantage may be lost and the situation reversed, with your side on the defensive. There are two more minds to cope with in doubles, and the quickest mind may get the jump by demoralizing one or other of the opponents and getting a lead before their team is well organized. Take the aggressive whenever you can.

Position in Doubles

It is difficult to say just where to stand in doubles. The play shifts so quickly that one should be on the move almost continually. Of course, command of the net position should be striven for at all times. When your partner is serving, it is rather easy for her to approach the net alongside of you either on the first or second shot. When an opponent is serving, you can stay up at the net, hoping your partner will make a good shot to follow in; or you can stay a little behind the service line, ready to follow her in with her shot. Side-by-side play is the safest for doubles nowadays. If one player is up and the other back, the opponents can usually force the play so as to win most of the rallies. When your partner is drawn out of court to play a shot, your position is in the center of the larger territory until a more normal position is possible. If you must take a lob over your partner's head, then she should cross over to your side of the court, and you should try to follow in to the net on your return. If you find it necessary to take a ball in front of your partner and near the center of the court, it is best to go back to your side afterwards. But if you should go close up to the net well over on her side, she should be ready to cross over and cover anything on your side. The angle of a return determines your proper position, so you should try to place your shots in such a location that the return will not come to a hole in your court. A quick piece of information helps here tremendously.

Teamwork

Many things can happen to change the scene and make teamwork necessary for a successful outcome in doubles. It should be a give-and-take proposition continually. Though one player usually dominates, the team will be stronger if this is not too pronounced and if the weaker player will take her full responsibility. She should give information quietly at every turn so that the master player will have less guesswork and can be more constructive. She must fit immediately into every situation, and must be quick to cover up her partner's court if it is vacated as a strategic move, and must not stop to think or say, "That was my shot." In my own case, when a partner surprises me by taking a shot which I had expected to play, my feet and mind automatically work even faster so as to be ready for the resulting shot. Do not be the kind of player who hits a shot and then sinks back onto her heels where she is and waits for another ball to come her way.

Follow the play alertly and move to the center of the territory where the next shot is likely to come. If your partner is drawn away out of court, you must try and be ready to cover more territory and give a decisive or defensive return, whichever is better, to allow your partner time to get back into position. A deep lob either to the back-court player or well over the girl at the net will often prove helpful. Be sure, however, that it is safe and deep.

Do not count on your opponents not being ready for a shot which is aimed right at either one. Many points are lost in that way, so take few chances and place your shots well away from them as a rule. Let the exceptions be when you make a mis-stroke or are forced into it.

The score sometimes determines when to take chances, but wait until you are a remarkable player before you take them, especially in doubles, where your partner is involved. Do not forget your partner at any time. Play for and with her continuously. You have part of the responsibility for making her play well. Encourage your partner to return every serve in such a way that the server will have to step to get it. A lob is disconcerting and easy to make and will accomplish this many times.

When you are out of position and off balance, do not try to make a shot which your partner could take. She may not have called but may be ready if you quickly call "Yours," and giver her plenty of room for hitting. When your partner calls "Mine" first, never play the ball unless you have a sure kill, because your partner has an aggressive shot in mind and has left her court unprotected to make it. It is hard to express in words the comfort there is in playing with a partner who helps at every stage. But how few such partners there are!

It is as true in tennis as in anything else that most people are inclined to blame others for their own mistakes. This is one of the difficulties to be overcome in doubles. Another is the common desire to win the point oneself. Team play is the answer, and the habit of giving information. In my own case, long experience makes me act almost automatically as soon as my opponent has hit the ball so that I am able to give information quickly and no shots have to be played hurriedly. But when I play with some partners who never call, my burdens are doubled. I have to think and act even faster. The rule should be to hurry the call and get to position but to be deliberate in making the shot. For instance, if your partner dislikes backhand shots, your anticipation of a ball on her backhand should be announced quickly by calling "Mine," or "I have it." This may make it possible for you to play an aggressive shot which you could not have made if you had waited for her to call for help at the last second. Should both players call at the same time, the one who played last should take the shot. Two heads and two racquets are better than one — if they work in unison.

A Word to Teachers

In teaching young children who have not had time to acquire poor form from imitation, few suggestions are necessary, especially if you can demonstrate skillfully yourself. If not, then it is best to have as many balls as you can collect in a basket and toss them to the child so that she can get them in as quick succession as possible. This is to develop the natural rhythmic motion of hitting and getting balanced for a return. On a later page are "Points to Remember" for practicing by oneself, either with or without a ball. Encourage any pupil to try them. A few phrases will often do wonders towards developing young players; for instance: "Shoulders up!" "Elbow up and out!" "Rest racquet!" "Skip!" "Don't cross foot over!" "Racquet behind ball!" "Don't drop racquet head!" "Get to position quickly!" "Watch the ball!" "Place your returns!" "Keep racquet back to the side, not behind you!"

Give plenty of opportunity for hitting all kinds of shots. Practice and the imitation of some good player are the best teachers. Of course, no two players play in exactly the same way. On that account it is wise to be flexible mentally as to grips, serves, and all strokes. A beginner, however, may want to use one stroke continually, and then it will be necessary to develop her interest by practice so that she will enjoy and use others. Stress rhythm and ease of motion around the court at all times. Developing competition in practice is a great help. This can be done by lining up groups of three to six children and giving them turns at hitting various shots. It is my practice to stand at the net and rally with several children, then do it with each one separately, counting strokes to see who is the best at keeping the ball in play. I then give them net practice. There are many such little ways of arranging competition within groups, all of which are beneficial.

Finally, it is important never to permit a beginner to drop a ball to hit; this will undo other good teaching which aims to instill the habit of holding the shoulders up and back. The hitting plane should be higher than it is apt to be when the ball is bounced, and the left hand and arm should always follow the rhythmic motion of the body.

In all this, I have tried to avoid technical language and to prove that it is simple to play good tennis if you are willing to go step by step, with faithful practicing, and to avoid imitation of unbalanced stroking. Champions are made through perseverance and the application of sound principles.

Appendix
Points to Remember

1. Stand alert, ready to start quickly, shoulders back, arms and racquet up.
2. Get well back and slightly to the side of the ball so that the head of the racquet will be behind it.
3. Just before hitting the ball, have your feet in line with the direction in which you are aiming.
4. Hit the ball as you shift your body weight from the back to the front foot.
5. Do not step onto your front foot. Just throw your weight onto it.
6. Rest your racquet at its throat between the thumb and the forefinger of your left hand and relax your right hand after every shot.
7. Get your weight onto your back foot and your racquet started up and back before removing your left hand.
8. As your weight is shifted to your right foot before forehand shots, your left hand and shoulder should start the left swing of the racquet, while your right arm and shoulder should be out and high. Then the muscles of your right arm and shoulder will not be needed until the forward swing.
9. Your right foot should start the forward swing with your right arm well out diagonally back to the side of the body for forehands in back-court play.
10. Volley with less of a swing back and forward of the racquet, but have your balance well in hand.
11. Let your right hand slide up the handle to the throat of your racquet as you walk around the court with the racquet held only by your right hand. This relieves strain and relaxes the muscles.
12. Never bounce the ball when starting a rally. Always toss it up and hit it on the fly, as in No. Eighteen below.
13. Practice hitting the ball against any space or wall. If the floor or ground is smooth, let the ball bounce before returning to the wall; if not, return the ball on the volley.

14. Start rallies easy and close to the bang-board with shortened grip, and increase speed and depth as control of the ball comes.
15. Develop footwork and anticipation by counting the number of times the ball is sent back and forth without missing and by trying to reach a certain number.
16. Have a definite object each time as to placing and timing.
17. Don't hit the ball off balance. Get near enough to avoid reaching. If you find you are too near, shorten your grip on the racquet before starting the forward swing to avoid stepping away from the ball as you hit.
18. Start a rally in this way: Step diagonally back onto the ball of your right foot, your right shoulder high and out, and your racquet up, out, back, and parallel to the net, your right hand halfway up the handle, your left hand well around to the side above your right foot. Stoop a little to gain momentum before tossing the ball up high above your right foot, while your racquet goes up, out, and farther back. Then push your weight from your right foot so that the impetus will travel through your body and the racquet will hit the ball alongside of you as your weight is being shifted to your left foot. Vary the height to which you toss the ball according to the amount of time you need to go back with your racquet, tossing it high if you want to hit the ball hard. All this is simpler than it sounds and will soon become second nature. Once mastered, it will make the difference between an erratic player and one that is easy and steady, with good control of every shot.

Slogans and Maxims

Games are for recreation. Enjoy your tennis.

Make excuses for others, never for yourself.

Results speak for themselves.

The better player usually wins. Strive to be better.

Errors lose most matches. Let your opponent make them.

Respect your opponent's ability.

Don't worry over your mistakes. Overcome them.

Don't reach and hit.

Don't step and hit.

A skip beats a step.

Skip before and after hitting.

Have momentum on tap.

Be a considerate winner and a cheerful loser.

Study your opponent's weaknesses.

Know your own limits. Use your strength to advantage.

Never find fault with racquet, court, or balls. Adjust yourself to circumstances.

Keep an open, cheerful mind.

The court is seventy-eight, not eighty-eight feet long.

The singles court is twenty-seven, not thirty seven feet long.

The net is three, not two feet high.

The net is to stop shots by your opponent. Aim your own over it and inside the court.

Mind makes a body wealthy; tennis keeps a body healthy.

Practice makes perfect.

A TENNIS ALPHABET

ALWAYS ALERT

BE BETTER

CONCENTRATE CONSTANTLY

DON'T DALLY

EVER EARNEST

FAIR FEELING

GET GOING

HIT HARD

IMITATE INSTRUCTOR

JUST JUMP

KEEP KEEN

LESS LOAFING

MOVE MEANINGLY

NEVER NET

ONLY OVER

PRAISE PARTNER

QUASH QUALMS

RELAX RIGHTLY

STAND STRAIGHT

TAKE TIME

UMPIRE USUALLY (on request)

VARY VOLLEYS

WORK WILES

XCEED XPECTATIONS

YELL YOURS

ZIP ZIP